A little course in...

Baking

A little course in...

Baking

DK

LONDON, NEW YORK, MUNICH,
MELBOURNE, DELHI

Senior Editor Alastair Laing
Project Art Editor Gemma Fletcher
Managing Editor Penny Warren
Managing Art Editor Alison Donovan
Senior Jacket Creative Nicola Powling
Jacket Design Assistant Rosie Levine
Pre-production Producer Sarah Isle
Producer Jen Lockwood
Art Directors Peter Luff, Jane Bull
Publisher Mary Ling

DK India
Senior Editor Garima Sharma
Senior Art Editor Ivy Roy
Managing Editor Alka Thakur Hazarika
Deputy Managing Art Editor Priyabrata Roy Chowdhury

Tall Tree Ltd
Editor Emma Marriott
Designer Ben Ruocco

Written by Amanda Wright

First published in Great Britain in 2013 by
Dorling Kindersley Limited, 80 Strand, London WC2R 0RL
Penguin Group (UK)

2 4 6 8 10 9 7 5 3 1
001–187845–Jan/2013

A CIP catalogue record for this book is available
from the British Library.

ISBN 978 1 4093 6521 1

Printed and bound by Leo Paper Products Ltd, China

Discover more at
www.dk.com

Contents

1
Start Simple

2
Build On It

3
Take It Further

Build Your Course

This book divides into broad sections that allow you to build a three-stage course in baking. All areas are covered, from quick cakes to artisan breads, with recipes that increase in difficulty to develop your skills base and set new challenges as you grow in confidence and experience.

From novice to master baker

Take your first steps with the recipes in Start Simple, which are easy to master and provide essential foundation skills. In Build On It you will discover many classic bakes and, once they are added to your repertoire, you can really call yourself a skilled baker. While the recipes in Take It Further have the "wow!" factor to stretch you and give you a chance to show off.

Recipe information

Symbols highlight the number of servings from each recipe, how long it takes to bake, and whether it can be frozen.

These details feature at the start of each recipe ┄┄►

Makes 18

Bakes in 10–15 minutes

Up to 8 weeks

Tip Boxes Crucial pieces of advice are highlighted in pullout boxes that will help you to achieve the best possible results.

┄ Clear photography demonstrates how to perform each technique correctly

How to **Pages**

Each area of baking is introduced on "How to" pages, which pinpoint the key techniques to understand before you tackle a recipe. Here we explain not only the "how?" but the "why?" as well, since understanding the reasons for doing something is crucial to getting it right.

1 After learning about the key techniques, these are then put into practice with an illustrated step-by-step recipe. A visual checklist of ingredients and special equipment, plus a detailed timeline, are included to help you plan.

Useful Advice Recipes are full of tips, reminders, warnings, and advice about what to do if things go wrong – like having a personal tutor helping out in the kitchen.

Annotations highlight what to do and how things should look at key stages

Achieving **Perfect Results**

At the end of each illustrated practice recipe, a realistic image of the finished bake demonstrates the results you should be aiming for.

Photographs show the right colour, texture, and decorative presentation you should try to match

Qualities to strive for with each bake are identified with annotations

Room for improvement?

Perfection can be difficult to achieve at the first attempt and below the image you will find common problems anticipated, explanations for

what probably went wrong, and advice for how to avoid making the same mistake next time.

Having mastered the practice recipe over the page you will find further similar recipes to enjoy.

Now turn over and start baking! ▶ ▶ ▶

Essential **Equipment**

MEASURING EQUIPMENT

Baking is a precise business and it's important to weigh and measure ingredients accurately. Scales are an absolute must, as are measuring jugs for liquids, measuring cups, which are essential for American recipes, and measuring spoons. Use either metric (g) or imperial (oz), but don't mix the two.

Scales
Accurate scales that weigh in small units are essential.

Measuring jug
For liquids. Jugs should measure both metric and imperial.

Measuring cups
American recipes measure by fractions of a cup.

Measuring spoons
For small quantities, from 1 tablespoon to ⅛ teaspoon.

MIXING EQUIPMENT

Basic mixing equipment should include different-sized mixing bowls and tools to sift, whisk, beat, combine, and fold in your ingredients.

Sieve
Sieving fine dry ingredients leaves them aerated and lump-free.

Wooden spoons
Strong and heat-resistant. For stirring, mixing, and creaming.

Large metal spoon
Bigger than a tablespoon, for folding in dry ingredients into cake mixtures.

Glass bowls
A selection of heavy-based, wide-brimmed bowls is invaluable for mixing, beating, and folding.

Hand and electric whisks
An electric whisk is essential, since it makes light work of any cake mix, as is a hand whisk for whisking egg whites, cream, or sauces.

Plastic spatula
Good for scraping out bowls and levelling and spreading mixtures.

PASTRY EQUIPMENT

Pastry-making requires some simple but vital tools for rolling and cutting dough into shapes, brushing on glazes or greasing tins, and baking pastry blind.

Pastry brush
For brushing water, egg wash, or glazes over desserts and bakes, or for greasing tins or trays.

Rolling pin
Essential for pastries, biscuits, and Danish pastries. Choose a heavy wooden rolling pin with handles for best results.

Baking beans
Used to fill a pastry case when baking it blind before adding the filling.

Pastry and cookie cutters
A basic selection should include round and fluted cutters, as well as individually shaped cutters.

TINS AND TRAYS

A good selection of tins, trays, and sheets are essential in baking. Always use the correct-sized tin and buy tins that are strong and sturdy.

Loaf tin
Ideal for bread as well as loaf-shaped cakes, and available in various sizes.

Baking trays and sheets
Various-sized baking trays, tins, and sheets will accommodate the different recipes you may want to make.

Tart tin
Loose-bottomed tart tins are essential for making sweet and savoury tarts and flans.

Round cake tins
Available in many sizes, loose-bottomed tins are perfect for cakes, and springform versions, which open at the side, are more suited to cheesecakes or delicate sponges.

Square cake tin
Perfect for cakes, bakes, and brownies, square tins have a fixed base.

Cupcake or muffin tin
A 12-hole tin for cupcakes or muffins. Muffin tins have deeper moulds.

ESSENTIAL EXTRAS

Metal skewer
A thin metal skewer is an essential tool to check your cakes are cooked properly.

Palette knife
A long, flexible blade with a round end, useful for smoothing surfaces and easing pastry from tins.

Wire rack
Keep at least one wire rack, ideally a large one, on which your bakes and cakes can cool.

Piping bag
A nylon piping bag with one plain and one star nozzle makes for a perfect, basic piping kit.

Baking parchment
For lining tins so the mix doesn't stick during baking, and to cover cakes if browning too much in the oven. Greaseproof paper is very similar and a good alternative.

Essential **Ingredients**

FLOUR

Flour is the key ingredient in most baking recipes. There are different types of flour, each containing varying levels of wheat grain and gluten, or added raising agent. Most baking recipes will require one or a mix of these flours.

Cornflour
A very fine flour made from the starch of maize kernels, typically used in shortbread for a light texture.

Plain flour
Contains 75% of the wheat grain and is used for many baking recipes, such as cakes, biscuits, and pastries.

Self-raising flour
Contains 75% of the wheat grain and an added baking agent to aid consistent rising in cakes and bakes.

Strong white bread flour
Made from durum wheat, with a higher protein and gluten content, making it perfect for bread.

Strong wholemeal bread flour
A nuttier flour made from milling the whole grain. Perfect for bread-making.

SUGAR

Sugar sweetens baked goods, but also adds moisture, colour, volume, and texture. It is available in different colours, from white to dark brown, and in varying granule size, from coarse to very fine. The type of recipe you make will dictate which type of sugar is best suited to it.

Soft brown sugar
Available in two varieties, light and dark, this moist, soft grain sugar is perfect for adding more flavour to cakes and bakes.

Muscovado sugar
A strongly flavoured, dark sugar that is perfect for fruit cakes.

Caster sugar
Widely used in baking, as its very fine crystals make it easy to mix in and dissolve.

Golden caster sugar
Very fine crystals with molasses left in for colour, and used in the same way as caster sugar.

Granulated sugar
Medium-sized sugar crystals work best for jam-making and decoration of cooked bakes and cakes.

Icing sugar
A fine white powdered sugar, made from grinding granulated sugar, and mostly used for icings and decoration.

DAIRY

Most baking recipes require fat, usually in the form of butter, to add essential flavour, volume, and a light texture. Other dairy products are also frequently used for different purposes, such as adding richness and moisture to a cake mix, for a smooth filling, or whipped up as decoration.

Butter
Available in unsalted and salted varieties, butter comes in block form and works best at room temperature for cakes and chilled for pastry.

Double cream
Adds richness and moistness, and is ideal for whipping to fill and decorate desserts.

Buttermilk
Often used with bicarbonate of soda, as the combination of the two acts as a raising agent.

Live natural yogurt
Adds moistness and also richness to baked recipes.

Mascarpone
A rich, silky-smooth Italian soft cream cheese, often used as an alternative to cream cheese.

Cream cheese
A soft, smooth cheese made with cream, most commonly used in cheesecakes.

ESSENTIAL EXTRAS

Eggs
Eggs add structure, moistness, flavour, and tenderness to baked goods and, unless otherwise specified, all recipes use medium eggs.

Chocolate
Used as chocolate chunks or cocoa powder; the higher the percentage of cocoa solids, the stronger the flavour.

Gelatine
A translucent, tasteless substance made from animal by-products. Used for setting fillings and jellies, it is available in leaf or powder form.

RAISING AGENTS

Raising agents ensure cakes and bakes rise during baking by producing bubbles of carbon dioxide when combined with heat, moisture, or acidity. These three raising agents are the most commonly used and are widely available.

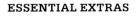

Baking powder
Produces carbon dioxide when combined with heat and warmth, and is widely used in baking.

Bicarbonate of soda
Produces carbon dioxide when combined with moisture and acidic products, such as buttermilk, treacle, or lemon juice.

Dried yeast
Most commonly used in bread, and needs careful preparation with heat and moisture to work properly.

1

Start Simple

It is time to put on your apron and get cooking with a selection of simple, step-by-step recipes and techniques to get you started in the world of baking. Learn how to make quick batter-style cakes and breads, light-as-air meringues, simple biscuits and cookies using the rubbed in and creaming methods, as well as creamy, crumbly cheesecakes and a first foray into pastry.

In this section, learn to bake:

Quick Cakes
pp.14–27

Cookies
pp.28–35

Biscuits
pp.36–43

Meringue
pp.44–55

No-bake Cheesecake
pp.56–63

Shop-bought Pastry
pp.64–71

Quick Breads
pp.72–79

How to make **Quick Cakes**

Quick cakes are the simplest cakes to make, as many of the processes used in traditional cake-making are left out: you simply mix to form a batter. Depending on the ingredients, there are various ways of making the batter. The easiest is the "all-in-one" method where everything is simply whisked together all at once. Common to all is the need to carefully combine wet and dry ingredients for a smooth batter with good volume.

Gently tap the edge of the sieve against your hand to help with the sieving process

Hold the sieve up as high as you dare to maximize contact with the air

Tip If you have time, sift the dry ingredients twice for a smoother, lighter mix.

Use a mixing bowl wider than the sieve to catch the flour

Sifting

Sift all your dry ingredients together through a sieve, holding the sieve high above the bowl. Sifting ingredients together mixes them, removes any lumps, and aerates the flour particles, which allows them to absorb liquids better and adds volume to the mix.

Pour the liquid into the well, then gradually draw the dry ingredients into the liquid

Create a well by drawing the dry ingredients out to the edges with your fingers or by using a wooden spoon

Mixing dry and wet ingredients

After whisking the wet ingredients until properly mixed, make a well in the centre of the flour mixture and pour in the liquid. A well helps to draw the dry ingredients into the wet ingredients a little at a time, so that you end up with a lump-free mixture. Alternatively, you can sift the dry ingredients into the wet ingredients and mix together.

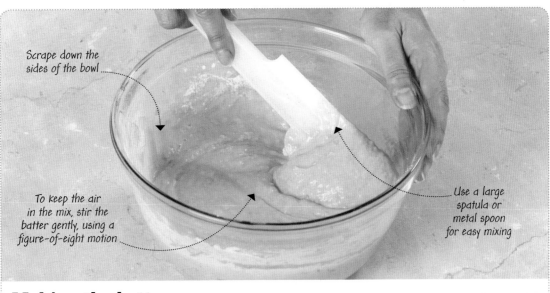

Scrape down the sides of the bowl

To keep the air in the mix, stir the batter gently, using a figure-of-eight motion

Use a large spatula or metal spoon for easy mixing

Making the batter

Using a spatula, gently mix the wet and dry ingredients together until no flecks of flour are visible. Do not overbeat the mixture, as this will cause the gluten in the flour to develop too much, and your cakes will end up on the heavy side.

Carrot Cake

This classic carrot cake is the ideal recipe to begin with.
Sift into your batter the dry ingredients and an array of
aromatic spices to make a deliciously moist and fruity
cake, topped with a silky smooth cream cheese icing.

Serves 8–10 **Bakes in 45 minutes** **Up to 8 weeks, un-iced**

Ingredients

For the cake

225ml (7½fl oz) sunflower oil, plus extra for greasing

3 large eggs

225g (8oz) soft light brown sugar

1 tsp vanilla extract

200g (7oz) carrots, peeled

100g (3½oz) walnuts

100g (3½oz) sultanas

200g (7oz) self-raising flour

75g (2½oz) wholemeal self-raising flour

pinch of salt

1 tsp cinnamon

1 tsp ground ginger

¼ tsp finely grated nutmeg

finely grated zest of 1 orange

For the icing

50g (1¾oz) unsalted butter, softened

100g (3½oz) cream cheese, at room temperature

200g (7oz) icing sugar

½ tsp vanilla extract

2 oranges

sunflower oil

eggs

brown sugar

Special Equipment

23cm (9in) springform cake tin

plain and wholemeal self-raising flour

carrots

vanilla extract

walnuts

sultanas

salt and spices

unsalted butter

cream cheese

icing sugar

oranges

springform cake tin

Total time *1 hour 15 minutes, plus cooling*

Prepare *10 minutes* **Make** *10 minutes* **Bake** *45 minutes* **Decorate** *10 minutes*

1 Preheat the oven to 180°C (350°F/Gas 4). Pour the oil and eggs into a large bowl along with the sugar and vanilla extract. Using an electric whisk, beat together until the mixture is slightly thickened.

Remember Ensure your ingredients are thoroughly mixed and smooth, otherwise you will have a lumpy cake.

Whisk until the sugar has dissolved and the mixture has thickened enough to drop heavily from the beaters

2 Finely grate the carrots, then place them in a clean tea towel, or you can use a piece of muslin. Tighten the tea towel around the grated carrot and squeeze tightly to remove excess liquid. Discard the liquid.

Why? You drain the liquid from the carrots so that the batter does not become too wet and the cake bakes properly.

3 Fold the carrot into the batter until well mixed. Scatter the walnuts on a baking tray and bake for 5 minutes in the preheated oven. Rub off their excess skin in a tea towel (see p.38). Roughly chop and stir the walnuts into the batter along with the sultanas.

Tip You don't have to bake the walnuts, but it helps when rubbing off their skins and enhances their flavour.

Do not overmix the cake batter or you will end up with a heavy cake

4 Sift the plain and wholemeal self-raising flours together with the salt, cinnamon, ginger, and nutmeg, adding any bran left in the sieve. Then stir in the orange zest and mix until all the ingredients are incorporated and no flecks of flour are visible.

Tip Make sure you sift the flour from a decent height in order to incorporate as much air as possible into the flour.

Make sure your bowl is large enough to catch the flour

5 Lightly oil the cake tin. Line the base of the tin with baking parchment by drawing a pencil round the outside of the tin on the parchment and then cutting it out. Spoon the cake mixture into the prepared tin and smooth the surface with a palette knife.

Why? Smoothing the batter at this stage helps the cake to bake with an even surface, making it easier to ice.

6 Bake the cake in the preheated oven for 45 minutes. Test if the cake is done with a skewer. Also it should be firm to the touch when gently pressed. Leave to cool in the tin for 5 minutes. Then move to a wire rack, so air can circulate around the cake, cooling it. Remove the baking parchment.

Remember Leave the cake to cool in the tin for 5 minutes so it is easier to turn it out of the tin.

A skewer inserted into the centre of the cake should come out clean

7 To make the icing, place the butter, cream cheese, sugar, and vanilla extract in a bowl, and grate in the zest of 1 orange. Using an electric whisk, beat the mixture until you get a smooth and silky mix.

Remember For a smooth icing, make sure the butter and cream cheese are at room temperature before blending.

Don't grate the bitter white pith, only the orange rind

Spread the icing over using a swirling motion for added texture

8 To decorate, spread the icing evenly over the cake with a palette knife. Using a zester, remove long decorative strands of rind from the other orange and sprinkle it around the edge of the cake. You can also use an ordinary grater, but the strands won't be as long.

Tip The iced cake will keep very well for up to 3 days in an airtight container.

The perfect **Carrot Cake**

Your cake should be firm, well risen, and moist, with evenly dispersed fruit and nuts.

Orange zest is sprinkled in a decorative ring

Icing is velvety smooth, and shiny

Crumb is moist, soft, and light

Sides of the cake are firm and dry to the touch

Fruit and nuts are evenly distributed throughout the cake

Did anything go wrong?

The cake is very heavy and dry. You may have overmixed the batter, which causes the gluten in the flour to develop, leading to a dry cake. Next time stop mixing as soon as you're confident the flour is mixed throughout.

There are specks of white flour in the cooked cake. You may not have sifted all lumps out of the flour or been careful enough during the mixing process to ensure no trace of flour remains.

The cake did not rise much. You may have overmixed the mixture, knocking the air out of the sponge. Mix only until all the ingredients are incorporated and no flecks of flour are visible.

The icing is running off the top of the cake. The cake was not cooled before you spread on the icing. Next time, be patient and give yourself enough time before icing.

The icing is lumpy. The butter and cream cheese may not have been at room temperature before you made the icing, causing lumps to form.

Try more Quick Cake recipes ▶ ▶ ▶

Banana Bread

**Makes
2 loaves**

**Bakes in
35–40
minutes**

**Up to
8 weeks**

Ingredients

unsalted butter for greasing

375g (13oz) strong white bread flour,
plus extra for dusting

2 tsp baking powder

2 tsp cinnamon

1 tsp salt

125g (4½oz) walnuts, coarsely chopped

3 ripe bananas, mashed

3 eggs, beaten

finely grated zest and juice of 1 lemon

120ml (4fl oz) vegetable oil

200g (7oz) granulated sugar

100g (3½oz) soft brown sugar

2 tsp vanilla extract

Special Equipment

2 x 450g (1lb) loaf tins

Preheat the oven to 180°C (350°F/Gas 4). Grease the loaf tins thoroughly and sprinkle 2 tablespoons of flour into each, shaking out any excess.

PREPARE THE BATTER

Sift the flour, baking powder, cinnamon, and salt into a bowl. Mix in the walnuts and make a well in the centre. Stir the bananas into the eggs with the lemon zest. Add the oil, sugars, vanilla extract, and lemon juice, and stir. Pour the banana mixture into the well in the flour. Gradually blend the dry ingredients in, stirring until just smooth.

Careful! Do not overmix the batter, otherwise your bread will be heavy.

BAKE THE BREAD

Spoon the batter into the prepared tins, dividing it equally. The tins should be about half full. Smooth over the surface, then bake in the oven for 35–40 minutes. Test each loaf by inserting a skewer into the centre. The bread is cooked if it comes out clean. If not clean, return to the oven for a further 5 minutes or so, and retest.

Remember When cooked, the loaves will start to shrink away from the sides of the tins.

SERVE THE BREAD

Leave the loaves to cool slightly in their tins, then transfer to a wire rack to cool completely. To serve, slice the bread and spread with butter or cream cheese. It is also good toasted.

Tip The bread will keep in an airtight container for up to 3 days.

Apple Muffins

Makes 12

Bakes in 20–25 minutes

Up to 8 weeks

Ingredients

1 Golden Delicious apple or other sweet dessert apple, peeled, cored, and diced

2 tsp lemon juice

115g (4oz) light demerara sugar, plus extra for sprinkling (optional)

200g (7oz) plain flour

85g (3oz) wholemeal flour

4 tsp baking powder

1 tbsp mixed spice

½ tsp salt

60g (2oz) pecan nuts, chopped

250ml (8fl oz) milk

4 tbsp sunflower oil

1 egg, beaten

Special Equipment

12-hole muffin tin

12 paper cases

Preheat the oven to 200°C (400°F/Gas 6). Line the muffin tin with paper cases.

PREPARE THE BATTER

Place the apple in a bowl with the lemon juice and 4 tablespoons of the sugar, and leave to soak for 5 minutes. Sift the plain and wholemeal flours, baking powder, mixed spice, and salt into a large bowl, adding in any bran left in the sieve. Add the remaining sugar and pecan nuts and make a well in the centre. In a jug, mix together the milk, oil, and egg, then stir in the apple mixture. Pour the wet ingredients into the dry ingredients and stir together until just mixed.

Careful! Stir the batter only till just mixed. Overmixing will result in heavy muffins.

Remember The batter will look lumpy at this stage, but this is normal.

BAKE THE MUFFINS

Spoon the batter into the prepared muffin cases, filling each three-quarters full. Bake in the oven for 20–25 minutes or until well risen and golden. Test by inserting a metal skewer into the centre of a muffin. If it comes out clean, they are cooked. If not, bake for another few minutes and test again. Leave the muffins to cool slightly before removing from their tin and transferring to a wire rack to cool completely. Sprinkle with a little extra sugar, if liked, before serving.

Tip These healthy muffins can be eaten warm or cold. They will keep fresh for up to 2 days if stored in an airtight container.

Ginger Cake

Serves 12

Bakes in 35–45 minutes

Up to 8 weeks

Ingredients

115g (4oz) unsalted butter, softened, plus extra for greasing

225g (8oz) golden syrup

115g (4oz) soft dark brown sugar

200ml (7fl oz) milk

4 tbsp syrup from jar of preserved ginger

finely grated zest of 1 orange

225g (8oz) self-raising flour

1 tsp bicarbonate of soda

1 tsp mixed spice

1 tsp cinnamon

2 tsp ground ginger

4 pieces of stem ginger, finely chopped and tossed in 1 tbsp plain flour

1 egg, lightly beaten

Special Equipment

18cm (7in) square cake tin

Preheat the oven to 160°C (325°F/Gas 3). Grease the cake tin and line the base with baking parchment.

PREPARE THE BATTER

Put the butter, syrup, sugar, milk, and preserved ginger syrup into a saucepan. Heat gently over a low heat until the butter has melted and the mixture is smooth and well mixed. Stir in the orange zest, remove from the heat, and leave to cool slightly for at least 5 minutes.

Sift together the flour, bicarbonate of soda, mixed spice, cinnamon, and ground ginger in a large mixing bowl.

Remember By sifting you are not only mixing, but also adding air into the batter, so don't miss out this step.

Make a well in the centre. Pour the melted mixture into the well and, using a balloon whisk, whisk together until all the ingredients are well mixed. Then stir in the preserved ginger and beaten egg. Pour the batter into the prepared tin.

BAKE AND SERVE

Bake in the preheated oven for 35–45 minutes or until a metal skewer inserted into the centre comes out clean. If not, return the cake to the oven, cook for a further 5 minutes, and retest. Leave the ginger cake to cool in its tin for at least 1 hour and then turn out onto a wire rack to cool completely.

Why? It's important to leave the cake to cool in its tin so it can firm up, making it less fragile and easier to remove from the tin.

Remove the baking parchment from the cake before cutting into 12 squares and serving.

Tip This cake is very moist, and will keep for up to 1 week in an airtight container.

Pecan, Coffee, and Maple Cake

Serves 8

Bakes in 35–40 minutes

Up to 8 weeks

Ingredients

225g (8oz) butter, softened, plus extra for greasing

225g (8oz) self-raising flour

175g (6oz) caster sugar

3 large eggs, at room temperature

4 tbsp espresso, or strong instant coffee

75g (2½oz) pecans, chopped, plus 20 pecan halves to decorate

1 tbsp maple syrup

200g (7oz) icing sugar

Special Equipment

2 x 18cm (7in) round cake tins

Preheat the oven to 180°C (350°F/Gas 4). Lightly grease the cake tins and line their bases with a circle of baking parchment.

PREPARE THE BATTER

Sift the flour into a large mixing bowl, then add the sugar, 175g (6oz) butter, eggs, and 2 tablespoons of the coffee. Whisk the ingredients together using an electric whisk until well mixed.

Remember The mixture should be of "dropping consistency", which means it should easily drop off the beaters when tapped.

Stir in the chopped pecan nuts.

Help! If the mixture seems a little thick, simply stir in a little extra coffee until it reaches the desired consistency.

BAKE THE CAKE

Divide the mixture between the tins, levelling the tops with a spatula or palette knife. Bake for 35–40 minutes or until well risen and firm to the touch. When the cakes are ready, a skewer inserted should come out clean. If not, cook for a further few minutes and retest. Leave to cool for 5 minutes in their tins, then transfer to a wire rack to cool completely.

DECORATE AND SERVE

To make the icing, melt the remaining butter and maple syrup in a small saucepan. Sift the icing sugar into a bowl, then add the melted butter mixture with the remaining coffee, and mix with the electric whisk until very thick and smooth. Using a spatula or palette knife, spread the coffee icing evenly between the tops of the cooled cakes for a smooth finish, then sandwich together and transfer to a serving plate. Decorate the top with the pecan halves.

Careful! The cakes must be completely cool or the icing will run.

How to make **Cupcakes**

Making small cakes, such as cupcakes, usually requires a very simple technique called "rubbing in". This involves rubbing the fat into the dry ingredients before whisking in the wet ingredients to form a smooth, pourable batter. The rubbing in process creates light cakes that have a soft texture.

Rubbing in the butter

Using your fingertips, rub the butter into the flour until the mixture looks like fine breadcrumbs. Rubbing in butter in this manner coats the flour with fat, without melting the butter too much. Coating the flour prevents too much gluten forming when you make the batter (see p.116), which in turn guarantees tender cakes.

Keep your palms facing up and use your fingertips to lift and rub the flour and butter together

Pour the same amount of batter into each cupcake case

Pouring

Once you have added the wet ingredients to the dry mixture, you will have a thick batter. For ease, pour the batter into a jug and then pour into paper cases placed in cupcake trays. Fill the cupcake cases half-full so the cakes rise evenly with flat tops. If you overfill them, the edges set faster during baking than the rest of the cake, causing the cakes to peak in the middle and crack.

Vanilla Cream Cupcakes

Makes 24

Bakes in 20–25 minutes

4 weeks, un-iced

Ingredients

200g (7oz) plain flour, sifted

2 tsp baking powder

200g (7oz) caster sugar

½ tsp salt

200g (7oz) unsalted butter, softened

3 eggs

150ml (5fl oz) milk

2 tsp vanilla extract

200g (7oz) icing sugar, sifted

sugar sprinkles, to decorate (optional)

Special Equipment

2 x 12-hole cupcake trays

piping bag and star nozzle (optional)

Preheat the oven to 180°C (350°F/Gas 4).

MAKE THE BATTER

In a bowl, place the flour, baking powder, sugar, salt, and half the butter. Rub in with your fingertips until the mixture resembles fine breadcrumbs. Whisk the eggs, milk, and 1 tsp of vanilla extract together until well blended. Slowly pour this mixture into the dry ingredients, whisking constantly, until you have a smooth batter. Pour the batter into a jug.

Remember It is very important to make a smooth batter, so always use softened butter and eggs at room temperature for easy mixing.

BAKE THE CUPCAKES

Place the cupcake cases into the cupcake trays, then pour the batter into the cases, filling each only half-full. Bake the cupcakes for 20–25 minutes until well risen. Insert a metal skewer into the centre of each cupcake. If it comes out clean each time, the cupcakes are ready. If not, simply cook for a further few minutes and test again. Leave the cakes to cool slightly, then remove them from the tin and transfer to a wire rack to cool completely.

DECORATE AND SERVE

To decorate, whisk the icing sugar with the remaining vanilla extract and butter, using an electric whisk, until light and fluffy. Spoon into a piping bag fitted with a star nozzle. Pipe the icing onto the cakes in a spiral pattern, starting at the edge and piping into the centre, ending with a peak. Decorate with sprinkles, if liked.

Tip You can also spoon the icing on the cupcakes instead of piping. Spread over the icing using the back of a spoon or a palette knife until smooth.

Chocolate and Lemon Cupcake variations
For chocolate cupcakes, sift 4 tbsp cocoa powder with the flour and stir 1 tbsp Greek yogurt in with the vanilla extract. For the icing, substitute 25g (1oz) cocoa powder for 25g (1oz) icing sugar. For lemon cupcakes, replace the vanilla extract in the batter with the zest of ½ lemon and juice of 1 lemon. Omit the vanilla in the icing and add the finely grated rind of ½ lemon instead.

How to make **Cookies**

The perfect cookie is golden brown in colour, with a soft middle and a slightly crisp outer edge. To achieve a light texture and to make sure that all the cookies in a batch turn out beautifully baked, it's vital to get air into the mix and to roll out the dough into evenly shaped balls.

A properly creamed mixture will be very smooth, lighter in colour, with a slightly increased volume

Whisk the butter and sugar together for 2-3 minutes until all the lumps have been smoothed out

Remember You can cream the ingredients by hand as well, using a wooden spoon, but it will take longer.

Creaming

This technique involves whisking the butter and sugar together until the mixture is light and fluffy. Creaming causes the sugar crystals to cut into the butter, creating pockets full of air, which will give your cookies a light texture on baking.

Make sure the nuts and raisins are properly combined, otherwise your cookies will have uneven amounts of filling

The dough should be soft but not sticky; add a little milk if too stiff or a little flour if too sticky

Achieving the correct consistency

To ensure a light, soft consistency to your dough, sift in the dry ingredients by holding the sieve high above the bowl and tapping it with your hand until all the flour falls into the bowl. Gently mix the ingredients together to make a dough that is soft but not sticky.

If the dough is a bit sticky, dust your hands with a little flour

Divide the dough into walnut-sized pieces and use the fingertips of one hand to roll into a ball in the palm of the other hand

Shaping the dough

Dividing and rolling the dough into equal-sized balls is an important part of making cookies. If you divide the dough into balls of varying sizes, you could end up with unevenly baked cookies, some that are underdone and others that are overcooked.

Hazelnut and Raisin Oat Cookies

For deliciously light and crumbly oat cookies flavoured
with raisins and hazelnuts, try this easy cookie recipe.
Perfecting the technique of making and shaping the dough
will give you perfectly baked cookies every time.

Makes 18 | Bakes in 10–15 minutes | Up to 8 weeks

Ingredients

100g (3½oz) hazelnuts

100g (3½oz) unsalted butter, softened

200g (7oz) soft light brown sugar

1 egg, beaten

1 tsp vanilla extract

1 tbsp runny honey

125g (4½oz) self-raising flour, sifted (see p.14)

125g (4½oz) jumbo porridge oats

pinch of salt

100g (3½oz) raisins

a little milk, if needed

hazelnuts

unsalted butter

soft light brown sugar

beaten egg

vanilla extract

honey

self-raising flour

jumbo porridge oats

salt

raisins

Total time *30–35 minutes, plus cooling*

Prepare
10 minutes

Make
10 minutes

Bake
10–15 minutes

1 Preheat the oven to 190°C (375°F/Gas 5). Toast the hazelnuts on a baking tray in the oven for 5 minutes, then rub off their skins using a clean tea towel and roughly chop.

Tip If preferred, and to save time, you can use ready-roasted chopped hazelnuts.

By crisping up the skins in the oven, they should now be easy to rub off

Adding honey will make the cookies extra moist

2 Place the butter and sugar in a large bowl and, using an electric whisk, cream them together until the mixture turns pale and fluffy. Add the egg, vanilla, and honey, and whisk again until thoroughly mixed.

Tip Ensuring your mixture is pale and fluffy will guarantee smooth-textured cookies.

3 Combine the flour, oats, and salt in a separate bowl, and stir into the mixture. Then stir in the chopped hazelnuts and raisins until everything is combined and distributed evenly.

Remember The cookie dough should be soft enough to shape but not sticky. Add a little extra milk if the mixture is too stiff or flour if too sticky.

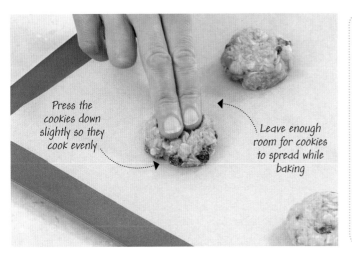

Press the cookies down slightly so they cook evenly

Leave enough room for cookies to spread while baking

4 Line a baking sheet with baking parchment. Roll the dough into 18 balls and flatten each slightly on the sheet. Bake in the preheated oven for 10–15 minutes or until golden. Transfer the cookies to a wire rack using a palette knife, and leave to cool.

Remember Try to make the balls as evenly sized as possible, so they cook consistently.

The perfect **Hazelnut and Raisin Oat Cookies**

Your baked cookies should be lightly golden brown, and softer in the middle with a light, chewy texture.

Did anything go wrong?

The cookies are too hard. You have baked them for too long. Remember that they firm up on cooling. Next time check them after 10 minutes and remove from the oven as soon as they look lightly golden.

The cookies are stuck together. The cookies were not spaced out enough prior to baking. Next time, allow more space between cookies for spreading.

Some of the cookies are cooked well, while others are too crispy. The dough was not shaped into even-sized balls.

The cookies are burnt around the edges, but not properly cooked in the centre. You did not flatten the cookies enough before baking.

The perfect cookie will have slightly crisp edges and a paler, softer centre

Try more Cookie recipes ▶ ▶ ▶

Pistachio and Cranberry Oat Cookies

Makes 24   **Bakes in 10–15 minutes**   **Up to 8 weeks**

Ingredients

100g (3½oz) pistachio nuts

100g (3½oz) unsalted butter, softened

200g (7oz) soft light brown sugar

1 egg

1 tsp vanilla extract

1 tbsp runny honey

125g (4½oz) self-raising flour, sifted

125g (4½oz) oats

pinch of salt

100g (3½oz) dried cranberries, roughly chopped

a little milk, if needed

Preheat the oven to 190°C (375°F/Gas 5). Line 2–3 baking sheets with baking parchment. Dry fry the pistachio nuts in a frying pan over a medium heat until lightly coloured, taking care not to let them burn. Leave to cool for 1 minute, then roughly chop.

Remember If you don't flatten the cookies slightly, they will cook unevenly and brown too much around the edges.

MAKE THE COOKIE DOUGH

Place the butter and sugar in a bowl and, using an electric whisk, mix together until smooth. Add the egg, vanilla extract, and honey, and whisk again until smooth. Stir in the flour, oats, and salt until well combined. Add the nuts and cranberries and mix well.

Help! If the dough is a little too stiff, add a small splash of milk to make it pliable.

SHAPE THE DOUGH

Divide the cookie dough into walnut-sized pieces (the size of whole walnuts, not walnut halves) and roll them into balls. Place on the baking sheets, leaving enough room for the cookies to spread when they cook, and flatten slightly.

BAKE THE COOKIES

In the preheated oven, bake the cookies in batches, one baking sheet at a time, for 10–15 minutes until golden brown. Leave the cookies on the sheets to cool and firm up slightly. Then, using a palette knife, transfer them to a wire rack to cool completely.

Tip The cookies will keep for up to 5 days if stored in an airtight container.

Apple and Cinnamon Cookies variation
Omit the nuts and cranberries and, after stirring in the flour and oats, add 2 teaspoons cinnamon and 2 peeled, cored, and finely grated apples.

Chocolate Chip Cookies

Makes 30

Bakes in approx. 30 minutes

Up to 8 weeks

Ingredients

200g (7oz) unsalted butter, softened
300g (10oz) caster sugar
1 large egg
1 tsp vanilla extract
300g (10oz) self-raising flour
150g (5½oz) dark or milk chocolate chips

Preheat the oven to 180°C (350°F/Gas 4). Line 2 baking sheets with baking parchment.

MAKE THE COOKIE DOUGH

Cream the butter and sugar together in a bowl using an electric whisk for 2–3 minutes until very pale and fluffy.

Remember Creaming brings air into the mix for a lighter cookie, so don't hurry this stage.

Stir in the egg and vanilla extract, then the flour, and beat together until the mixture forms soft dough. Stir in the chocolate chips until well mixed.

Careful! Make sure you mix the chocolate chips evenly throughout the dough so that no cookies are short of chips.

SHAPE THE DOUGH

Divide the cookie dough into walnut-sized pieces (the size of whole walnuts, not walnut halves), shaping in the palms of your hands. Arrange the dough balls on the prepared baking sheets, leaving enough space around each ball, as they spread during baking. Flatten the dough balls very slightly.

Help! If the dough is a little sticky, use lightly floured hands for easier handling.

BAKE THE COOKIES

In the preheated oven, bake the cookies in 2 batches, for 12–15 minutes each or until golden. Leave the cookies to cool slightly on their baking sheets, then transfer to a wire rack to firm up, using a palette knife, and cool completely.

Remember Don't worry if the cookies are a little soft when you take them out of the oven. They will firm up further on cooling.

Tip These cookies are equally delicious whether served warm or cold. They will keep for up to 5 days if stored in an airtight container.

How to make **Biscuit Dough**

Biscuit dough is simple to make and once mastered, you can cut it
into a variety of shapes or add an extra flavouring or two. It's important
to achieve a fine consistency when rubbing the butter into the flour and
also to roll the dough out into a thin, even layer.

Rub the butter and flour together between your fingertips until the mix has the consistency of fine breadcrumbs

Remember The finer the crumbs, the more tender your biscuits will bake.

Use only your fingertips to rub in so that the butter doesn't start melting

Rubbing in

Rubbing the butter into the flour helps to coat
the flour particles, which in turn prevents
gluten forming, keeping the biscuits deliciously
"short" or crisp and crumbly. The dough
is then very gently kneaded, just enough to
bring it together and smooth out any cracks.

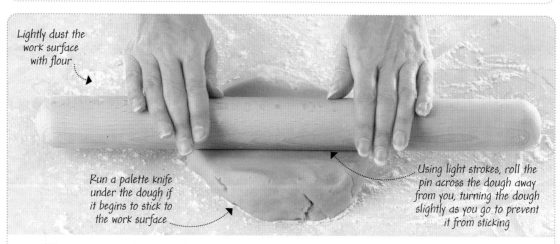

Lightly dust the work surface with flour

Run a palette knife under the dough if it begins to stick to the work surface

Using light strokes, roll the pin across the dough away from you, turning the dough slightly as you go to prevent it from sticking

Rolling out the dough

Scatter flour over the surface and on the rolling
pin so the dough doesn't stick. Place the flat of
your hands on each end of the rolling pin, then
gently roll the dough away from you, using long
strokes until the dough is 5mm (¼in) thick all
over. This ensures all the biscuits cook evenly.

How to make **Shortbread**

Shortbread is a rich and crumbly type of biscuit that can be made into traditional wedges, biscuits, or fingers. The high butter content gives shortbread its characteristically crumbly or "short" texture, and the key to its success is not to overwork the dough.

Making the dough

As there are no raising agents in shortbread dough, you need to cream together the butter and sugar (see p.28) in order to get air into the mixture. You then gently mix in the other ingredients to form a crumbly looking dough.

Don't overmix, otherwise the shortbread will lose its crumbly texture and become tough

Don't worry if your dough is a bit crumbly at this stage

Shaping the dough

When the dough is ready, shape it into a rough ball without kneading it. You want the shortbread to have a light and crumbly texture. Kneading would overwork the gluten in the flour, making it tough.

Scoring the dough

Once you have pressed the dough flat in a baking tin, use a sharp knife to "score" or lightly mark it into wedges. This makes it easier to cut or break the shortbread into wedges once it is baked. Then prick it all over with a fork.

Pricking the shortbread all over allows steam to escape as it cooks and prevents it from rising up, leaving a level surface

Butter Biscuits

To make quick and easy biscuits using the
"rubbed in" method, why not try this simple recipe
for deliciously light and crumbly butter biscuits.

Makes 30

Bakes in 10–15 minutes

Unsuitable for freezing

Ingredients

150g (5½oz) unsalted butter, softened and diced

225g (8oz) plain flour, sifted (see p.14), plus extra for dusting

100g (3½oz) caster sugar

1 egg yolk

1 tsp vanilla extract

Special Equipment

7cm (2¾in) round pastry cutter

unsalted butter

plain flour

caster sugar

egg yolk

vanilla extract

round pastry cutter

Total time *25–30 minutes, plus cooling*

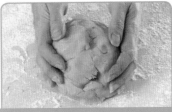

Prepare
5 minutes

Make
10 minutes

Bake
10–15 minutes

1 Preheat the oven to 180°C (350°F/Gas 4). Using your fingertips, rub together the butter, flour, and sugar, until they resemble fine breadcrumbs. Using a wooden spoon, mix in the egg yolk and vanilla extract. You may not need all the egg yolk, just enough to form a soft, but not sticky, dough.

Tip To save time, blitz the flour and butter together in a food processor to form the breadcrumbs.

Dough should be soft and still a little crumbly

Do not add too much flour to the surface, as this will make the biscuits dry

2 Form the dough into a ball, then turn it out onto a lightly floured surface. Knead the dough for a few seconds with the heel of your hand. Push it forward slightly, then fold its far edge into the centre. Turn the dough and repeat the process until the dough is smooth.

Help! If your dough is a bit too soft and sticky to roll out, chill it for 15 minutes, and then try again.

3 To roll out the dough, start by slightly flattening the it with your hand. Then, using the rolling pin, gently roll it out, without applying too much pressure. Roll the dough only in one direction, away from your body. Continue to roll the dough out to a thickness of 5mm (¼in).

Tip To prevent the dough from sticking to the work surface, run a palette knife under it.

Roll the dough out using long strokes going away from you so you get an even thickness

4 Using a pastry cutter, cut out 30 rounds of the dough, bringing together and re-rolling any leftover dough so you get the maximum number of biscuits. Place them on baking sheets; you don't need to grease or line the sheets. Bake for 10–15 minutes or until golden brown at the edges. Leave to cool slightly, then transfer to a wire rack to cool completely.

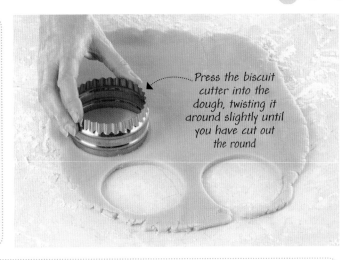

...Press the biscuit cutter into the dough, twisting it around slightly until you have cut out the round

The perfect **Butter Biscuit**

The perfectly baked butter biscuit will be lightly golden in colour and have a crisp and crumbly texture. They will keep well for up to 5 days if stored in an airtight container.

The biscuits should be golden at the edges and slightly paler in the centre...

Did anything go wrong?

The biscuit dough was very sticky. You may have added a little too much egg yolk. Next time, add just enough to bind the ingredients together, and don't be afraid to leave out any surplus.

The biscuits have joined at the edges on baking. You may not have left enough space on the baking sheet between the rounds to allow them to spread during baking.

The biscuits are very dry. You may have put too much flour on your work surface while rolling out the dough.

The edges of the biscuits have browned too much. You may have overcooked them. Next time, take them out of the oven when they start to turn lightly golden at the edges.

I didn't manage to get 30 biscuits from the dough. You may not have rolled the dough out thinly enough. Did you remember to re-roll any leftover dough?

Try more Biscuit recipes ▶ ▶ ▶

Gingerbread Men

Makes 16

Bakes in 10–12 minutes

Up to 8 weeks, unbaked

Ingredients

4 tbsp golden syrup

300g (10oz) plain flour, plus extra for dusting

1 tsp bicarbonate of soda

1½ tsp ground ginger

1½ tsp mixed spice

100g (3½oz) unsalted butter, softened and diced

150g (5½oz) soft dark brown sugar

1 egg

raisins, to decorate

icing sugar, sifted (optional)

Special Equipment

11cm (4½in) gingerbread man cutter

Preheat the oven to 190°C (375°F/Gas 5).

MAKE THE DOUGH

Gently heat the syrup in a small saucepan until it is runny, then leave to cool slightly.

Careful! Don't neglect to cool the syrup or it will start to cook the egg and melt the butter.

Sift together the flour, bicarbonate of soda, ginger, and mixed spice. Add the butter and rub in till resembles fine crumbs (see p.26). Stir in the sugar. Beat the egg into the cooled syrup and pour into the dry ingredients. Mix together with a spoon and then your hands to form dough.

SHAPE THE DOUGH

Briefly knead the dough on a floured surface until smooth. Roll out to 5mm (¼in) thickness.

Careful! Don't put too much flour on your work surface when rolling the dough out, otherwise the biscuits will be dry.

Using the cutter, cut out as many gingerbread men as you can. Re-roll the leftover dough and cut out more gingerbread men. Transfer the men to non-stick baking sheets and use raisins to make their eyes, noses, and buttons.

BAKE AND DECORATE

Bake for 10–12 minutes or until golden brown. Cool slightly, then transfer them to a wire rack to cool completely. The gingerbread men will firm up a lot on cooling, so do not overbake them or they will be too crispy.

To decorate, mix a little icing sugar with enough water to form a thin icing. Decorate the men with the icing to make their clothes and bow ties. Leave the icing to set completely.

Shortbread

Makes 8 triangles

Bakes in 30–40 minutes

Unsuitable for freezing

Ingredients

150g (5½oz) unsalted butter, softened, plus extra for greasing

75g (2½oz) caster sugar, plus extra for sprinkling

175g (6oz) plain flour

50g (1¾oz) cornflour

Special Equipment

18cm (7in) loose-bottomed round cake tin

Lightly grease and line the tin with baking parchment.

MAKE THE DOUGH

Combine the softened butter and the sugar in a bowl, then cream together using an electric whisk for 2–3 minutes or until very light and fluffy. Sift the flour and cornflour into the bowl and mix. Using your hands, bring the mixture together to form a dough, then place in the tin.

Remember At this stage, the dough will be slightly crumbly.

Careful! Do not overwork the dough, otherwise your shortbread won't be light and crumbly.

SHAPE THE DOUGH

Press the dough into the tin using your hands, until it fills the tin and is smooth and even on top. Using a sharp knife, lightly score the shortbread into 8 even wedges. Prick the shortbread all over with a fork, then cover it with cling film and chill in the fridge for 1 hour. Preheat the oven to 160°C (325°F/Gas 3).

BAKE THE DOUGH

Bake the shortbread in the preheated oven for 30–40 minutes until lightly golden and firm.

Careful! Keep an eye on the shortbread in case it starts to colour too much; if it does, lightly cover with foil.

Re-score the wedges using a sharp knife while the shortbread is still warm. Sprinkle a dusting of caster sugar over the top and leave to cool completely. When cool, carefully remove from the tin. Break or cut the shortbread into wedges along the scored lines and serve.

Tip Shortbread will keep well for up to 5 days if stored in an airtight container.

How to make **Meringue**

Meringues are made by whisking lots of air into egg whites, then whisking in sugar. The mixture is then shaped and baked slowly on a low heat so that the moisture in the mixture evaporates, leaving you with crisp meringues that are light as air.

To ensure your bowl is completely clean, run half a lemon around the bowl before using

Remember to scrape down the sides of the bowl occasionally using a plastic spatula

The egg whites are ready when you lift out the whisk and it leaves behind peaks of egg white that hold their shape

Careful! The egg whites must be free from any grease or egg yolk, otherwise they won't whisk to a stiff peak. Also take care when separating the eggs so you don't burst the yolk and contaminate the whites.

Whisking the egg whites

For a light and crisp meringue, you must whisk your egg whites vigorously using an electric whisk. This stretches the protein in the egg whites, which helps to incorporate air into the mix and, as a result, increase the volume in the egg whites.

Careful! If you add the sugar before the egg whites are stiff enough, your meringue will end up too soft.

The whisked egg whites will become smoother and glossier with every addition of sugar

The meringue will form stiff glossy peaks when ready

Stop whisking when your mixture is smooth and glossy

Whisking in the sugar

Using an electric whisk, beat in a spoonful of sugar at a time; any quicker and you may deflate the mixture. Take care to dissolve the sugar into the egg whites by whisking very well after each addition. The mixture will no longer feel grainy when the sugar has fully dissolved. Undissolved sugar attracts moisture, making the meringue soggy.

Strawberry Pavlova

This scrumptious strawberry pavlova combines juicy,
sharp strawberries with crisp, sweet meringue. It's an
impressive-looking dessert, but easy to make once you've
mastered the basic meringue technique. It can also be
prepared in advance of a dinner party and assembled
just before serving.

Serves 8

Bakes in 1 hour 20 minutes

Unsuitable for freezing

Ingredients

6 egg whites, at room temperature

pinch of salt

approx. 360g (12½oz) caster sugar (see tip, Step 1)

2 tsp cornflour

1 tsp white wine vinegar

300ml (10fl oz) double cream

strawberries, hulled and halved, to decorate (or other fruits)

egg whites

salt

caster sugar

cornflour

white wine vinegar

double cream

strawberries

Total time *1 hour 40 minutes, plus cooling*

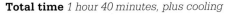

Prepare
5 minutes

Make
10 minutes

Bake
1 hour 20 minutes

Decorate
5 minutes

1 Preheat the oven to 180°C (350°F/Gas 4). Line a baking sheet with parchment paper and draw a 20cm (8in) circle with a pencil, using an upturned plate as guide. Whisk the egg whites and salt until they form stiff peaks.

Tip You will need exactly double the weight of sugar to egg whites. Before you start whisking, weigh your 6 egg whites and calculate exactly how much sugar you need.

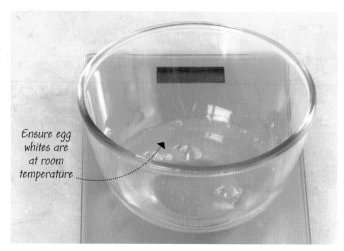

Ensure egg whites are at room temperature

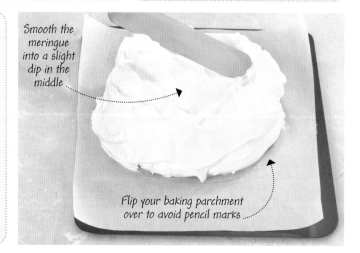

Use a glass or metal bowl when making the meringue, as plastic can retain traces of grease

2 Gradually add the sugar, a spoonful at a time, whisking well after each addition. Continue whisking until the whites are stiff and glossy, then whisk in the cornflour and vinegar.

Why? Cornflour and vinegar add a softer, chewier texture and stop the egg whites from collapsing.

Careful! Add the sugar gradually, else the meringue will be soft.

3 Spoon the meringue into a mound inside the circle on the lined baking sheet. First spoon it into the middle, then spread it out to the guideline using a palette knife. Texture the meringue into neat decorative swirls. Bake in the oven for 5 minutes, then reduce to 130°C (250°F/Gas ½) and cook for a further 75 minutes until the meringue is crisp and dry. Leave to cool completely in the oven.

Smooth the meringue into a slight dip in the middle

Flip your baking parchment over to avoid pencil marks

4 Meanwhile, lightly whip the cream using an electric whisk until it just holds its shape. Arrange the cooled meringue on a serving plate, spoon the cream onto the centre, leaving a rim around the edge, top with the strawberries, and serve.

Careful! Top the meringue with the cream and strawberries just before you serve, otherwise the meringue will soften.

..Whisk the cream until it just forms soft peaks or it will be too firm to spread

The perfect **Strawberry Pavlova**

Your finished pavlova should be crisp and creamy white with a soft and chewy centre.

Did anything go wrong?

The egg whites won't whisk to a stiff peak. Egg yolk or oil from unwashed cooking equipment has got into your egg whites.

The meringue mixture has not got much volume to it. You may have added the sugar before whisking the egg whites into stiff peaks.

The meringue has sunk on cooling. It is always best to leave the meringue to cool down completely in the turned-off oven, thus preventing a sudden change in temperature that could cause the meringue to sink or crack.

The meringue has softened. You may have assembled the pavlova too early or spread the cream too widely over the meringue. Next time, assemble just before serving and leave a rim around the edge to prevent the sides softening and collapsing.

Softly whipped cream

Crisp meringue with few cracks

Try more Meringue recipes ▶ ▶ ▶

Tropical Fruit Pavlova

Serves 8

Bakes in 1 hour 20 minutes

Unsuitable for freezing

Ingredients

6 egg whites, at room temperature

pinch of salt

approx. 360g (12¼oz) caster sugar (see tip)

2 tsp cornflour

1 tsp vinegar

300ml (10fl oz) double cream

400g (14oz) mango and papaya, peeled and chopped

2 passion fruits, halved

Preheat the oven to 180°C (350°F/Gas 4). Line a baking sheet with parchment and, using a pencil, draw a 20cm (8in) circle on it. Flip the paper over so the pencil does not mark the meringue.

Tip Before you begin to make the pavlova, weigh your 6 egg whites and use exactly double the weight of sugar.

MAKE THE MERINGUE

Put the egg whites in a large, clean, grease-free bowl with the salt. Using an electric whisk, whisk the egg whites until stiff peaks form. Add the sugar 1 tablespoon at a time, whisking well after each addition. Continue whisking until the mixture becomes very stiff and glossy. Then whisk in the cornflour and vinegar.

Why? Adding cornflour and vinegar to the mix gives the meringue's centre a chewy texture, while its outside remains crisp.

SHAPE AND BAKE THE MERINGUE

Spoon the meringue inside the drawn circle on the baking parchment and spread out with a palette knife. Bake for 5 minutes, then reduce the oven temperature to 130°C (250°F/Gas ½), and cook for 1¼ hours. The meringue is cooked when it is crisp and dry. At this point turn off the oven and, without opening the door, leave the meringue inside until it has completely cooled.

Careful! Don't be tempted to open the oven door before the meringue has cooked, otherwise it will deflate and crack.

DECORATE AND SERVE

Whip the double cream in a bowl, using an electric whisk, until it holds its shape. Remove the pavlova from the parchment and arrange on a serving plate. Just before serving, top the pavlova with the whipped cream, then arrange the prepared fruits on top. Spoon the passion fruit juice and seeds over the top to finish, and serve.

Tip The meringue base will keep very well if stored in an airtight container for up to 1 week. Always add any toppings to a pavlova just before serving to prevent it from turning soggy.

Rhubarb and Ginger Meringue Cake

Serves 6–8

Bakes in 1 hour 5 minutes

Unsuitable for freezing

Ingredients

4 egg whites, at room temperature

pinch of salt

325g (11oz) caster sugar

600g (1lb 5oz) rhubarb, chopped

4 pieces of stem ginger, chopped

½ tsp ground ginger

250ml (8fl oz) double cream

icing sugar, to dust

Preheat the oven to 180°C (350°F/Gas 4). Line 2 baking sheets with baking parchment and draw an 18cm (7in) circle with pencil on each of them. Flip the paper over so the pencil does not mark the meringue.

MAKE THE MERINGUE

Put the egg whites and salt in a large grease-free bowl. Using an electric whisk, whisk the egg whites until very stiff peaks form. Add 225g (8oz) of the sugar, 1 tablespoon at a time, whisking well after each addition until all is incorporated and the mixture is stiff and glossy.

Remember Don't add your sugar before the egg whites are whisked to stiff peaks, otherwise the meringue will be soft.

SHAPE AND BAKE THE MERINGUE

Divide the meringue between the baking sheets and spread out to the circle guidelines. Cook the meringue for 5 minutes, then reduce the oven temperature to 130°C (250°F/Gas ½). Bake for 1 hour, then turn off the oven and leave the meringue to cool completely.

Why? Allowing the meringue to cool slowly in the turned-off oven prevents the meringue from cracking too much.

ASSEMBLE AND SERVE

Put the rhubarb, remaining sugar, stem ginger, and ground ginger in a saucepan and add just enough water to cover. Cook gently with the lid on for 20 minutes or until soft. Drain off any excess liquid, allow it to cool, and chill till required. Whisk the double cream in a bowl, using an electric whisk, until it holds its shape. Then fold in the chilled rhubarb mix. Remove the meringue from the parchment and place one round on a serving plate. Spread the rhubarb and ginger filling on top and place the other meringue over it. Dust the top of the meringue cake liberally with icing sugar. Cut into slices and serve immediately.

Tip The meringue layers will keep very well if stored in an airtight container for up to 5 days. Assemble the cake just before serving to prevent it from becoming soggy.

How to **Pipe Meringue**

You can pipe meringue into rounds, fingers, or even large, flat discs for layered desserts. You can also spoon meringue into your chosen shapes, but piping is faster, gives a more professional finish, and is less messy once you've mastered it. To spoon meringue into shapes, take two dessert spoons, scoop out enough meringue to shape between the spoons, and form the meringue into your desired shape.

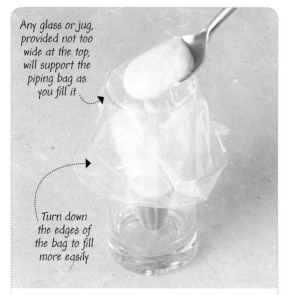

Any glass or jug, provided not too wide at the top, will support the piping bag as you fill it

Turn down the edges of the bag to fill more easily

After piping each round, press down the nozzle very gently into the top of the meringue to prevent it forming a peak

Leave space between each round for spreading

Filling the piping bag

Fit your piping bag with a plain or star nozzle, then place it in a glass for support. Spoon your meringue into the piping bag and, when done, twist the top of the bag to keep the meringue in place.

Piping rounds of meringue

Hold the piping bag with one hand at the top and, using the other hand to guide it, gently squeeze the meringue through the nozzle. Hold the nozzle still until you form a rounded pile of meringue on a lined baking tray.

Piping meringue into a disc

To create a large, flat disc of meringue, pipe in a spiral, about 1cm (½in) thick. Start from the centre and work outwards to your required size.

Make a circle guideline on baking parchment and mark a cross at the centre of the circle to start from

Raspberry Cream Meringues

Makes 6–8	**Bakes in 1 hour**	**Unsuitable for freezing**

Ingredients

4 egg whites, at room temperature

approx. 240g (8¾oz) caster sugar (see tip)

100g (3½oz) raspberries

300ml (10fl oz) double cream

1 tbsp icing sugar, sifted

Special Equipment

piping bag and plain nozzle

Preheat the oven to 130°C (250°F/Gas ½). Line 2 baking sheets with baking parchment.

Tip Weigh out the egg whites and calculate how much sugar you need before starting. You will need double the weight of sugar to egg whites.

WHISK THE MERINGUE

Put the egg whites in a large, clean, grease-free bowl and, using an electric whisk, beat the egg whites until very stiff peaks form. Gradually add half the sugar, a couple of tablespoons at a time, whisking well after each addition. Gently fold in the remaining sugar until all is incorporated.

Careful! Make sure the sugar is whisked in gradually, otherwise the meringue will be soft.

SHAPE AND BAKE

Pipe rounds onto the lined baking sheets using the piping bag fitted with a plain nozzle. Leave a 5cm (2in) gap between each round. Alternatively, spoon dessert spoons of the mixture onto the sheets. Bake in the preheated oven for 1 hour. Turn off the heat and leave the meringues inside the oven to cool completely, leaving the door shut.

Remember The meringues will be crisp and dry when cooked and should sound hollow when tapped on their base.

FILL AND SERVE

Crush the raspberries with a fork in a bowl. Whisk the double cream in another bowl using an electric whisk until it holds its shape and then stop as you don't want to overwhisk it. Gently fold the crushed raspberries and icing sugar into the cream until well mixed. When ready to serve, spread a little of the raspberry mixture onto half of the meringues. Top with remaining meringues and press together. Serve immediately.

Tip Unfilled meringues will keep very well for up to 5 days if stored in an airtight container. Always assemble the meringues just before serving to prevent them becoming soggy.

Brown Sugar Meringues

Makes 18

Bakes in 1 hour

Unsuitable for freezing

Ingredients

4 egg whites, at room temperature

200g (7oz) soft brown sugar

300ml (10fl oz) double cream

85g (3oz) dark chocolate, broken into pieces

Special Equipment

piping bag and plain nozzle

Preheat the oven to 130°C (250°F/Gas ½). Line 2 baking sheets with baking parchment.

MAKE THE MERINGUE

Put the egg whites in a large, clean, grease-free bowl. Whisk the egg whites, using an electric whisk, until very stiff peaks form.

Careful! Always make sure your bowl and whisks are totally free from any grease or egg yolk. Even a tiny trace could prevent the air from being incorporated properly and stop the egg whites whisking up enough.

Gradually add the sugar, 2 tablespoons at a time, and whisk well after each addition, until all is incorporated. Continue to whisk until the mixture is very thick and glossy.

SHAPE AND BAKE

Pipe rounds onto the lined baking sheets using the piping bag fitted with a plain nozzle. Leave a 5cm (2in) gap between each round. Alternatively, spoon dessert spoons of the mixture onto the sheets. You should end up with 36 meringues. Bake in the preheated oven for 1 hour. To ensure the meringues stay crisp, turn off the oven and leave the meringues to cool inside. Then transfer them to a wire rack to cool completely.

Remember The meringues will be crisp and dry when cooked and should sound hollow when tapped on their base.

DECORATE AND SERVE

Whisk the double cream in a bowl, using an electric hand whisk, until it holds its shape. Melt the chocolate until smooth in a heatproof bowl set over a pan of simmering water.

Careful! Do not let the base of the bowl containing the chocolate touch the water, otherwise the chocolate will overheat and go grainy.

When ready to serve, spread a little of the whipped cream onto half of the meringues. Top with the remaining half of the meringues and press together. Arrange the brown sugar meringues on a serving plate. Using a teaspoon, carefully drizzle a little of the melted chocolate over each meringue and serve immediately.

Pistachio Meringues

Makes 8

Bakes in 1½ hours

Unsuitable for freezing

Ingredients

100g (3½oz) unsalted, shelled pistachio nuts

4 egg whites, at room temperature

approx. 240g (8½oz) caster sugar (see tip)

Preheat the oven to 130°C (250°F/Gas ½). Line a baking sheet with baking parchment.

Tip Weigh the egg whites and calculate how much sugar is needed. You will need double the weight of sugar to egg whites.

PREPARE THE NUTS

Put the pistachio nuts on an unlined baking sheet and bake for 5 minutes, then place on a clean tea towel and rub to remove their skins. Finely grind half the nuts in a food processor and roughly chop the rest.

WHISK THE MERINGUE

Put the egg whites in a large, clean, grease-free bowl and, using an electric whisk, beat until very stiff peaks form. Gradually add the sugar, 2 tablespoons at a time, whisking well after each addition, until half of the sugar is incorporated. Fold in the remaining sugar and ground pistachio nuts very carefully.

Remember Fold in the sugar and ground pistachio nuts very carefully making sure you do not knock any air out of the mixture, which could deflate the meringue.

SHAPE AND BAKE

Place heaped tablespoons of the meringue onto the lined baking sheet, placing them well apart as they will spread as they bake. Scatter

the tops with the chopped pistachio nuts. Bake the meringues for 1½ hours, or until crisp and dry, then turn off the oven and leave the meringues inside to cool completely. This will help to minimize the amount of cracking.

Tip These meringues will keep very well if stored in an airtight container for up to 3 days.

How to make **No-Bake Cheesecake**

No baking is required for these quick cheesecakes, as the cream cheese filling is set with gelatine. Gelatine is an easy-to-use gelling agent made from animal protein, which is supplied in powdered form or in transparent leaves. The velvety texture of the topping, beaten until very smooth, contrasts beautifully with the crispy crumb base.

The biscuits for the base need to be finely crushed, else the base will break up easily and won't support the cheesecake

Press down the biscuit crumb mixture firmly with the back of a spoon to form an even base

Tip You can use most types of biscuits for the base. To save time, you can also crush the biscuits in a food processor.

Making the base

The classic biscuit base is made by mixing biscuit crumbs with melted butter, then pressing the mix into the tin. On chilling, the butter solidifies and binds the crumbs into a firm base to support the cream cheese filling. To make the base, place the biscuits in a freezer bag and crush with a rolling pin until they resemble fine breadcrumbs (see p.106).

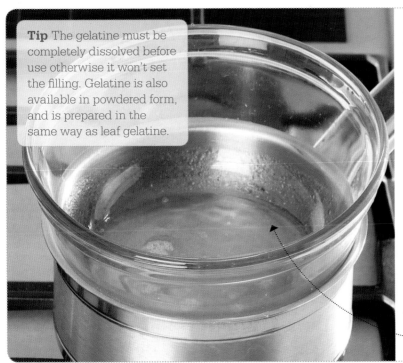

Tip The gelatine must be completely dissolved before use otherwise it won't set the filling. Gelatine is also available in powdered form, and is prepared in the same way as leaf gelatine.

Dissolving the gelatine

Leaf gelatine must be cut into pieces and soaked in a liquid before use. This softens the gelatine, allowing it to absorb water and dissolve fully when melted over a pan of simmering water. As it melts, stir until no traces of the gelatine are visible. Cool for 3–5 minutes before adding to the filling. The gelatine will then re-form into a gel that sets the topping.

...Dissolved gelatine will form a clear, smooth liquid

Making the filling

A typical filling is a mix of whipped cream and cream cheese or similar alternatives such as mascarpone or ricotta cheese. The key to a great filling is to beat the cream cheese until very smooth and then gently fold in the whipped cream using a figure-of-eight movement, to ensure you don't lose any volume.

Ensure the cream cheese is at room temperature before beating for a lump-free filling...

Lemon Cheesecake

Try this simple but luscious lemon cheesecake recipe.
It combines a perfectly smooth filling on a crispy biscuit
base. An all-time favourite, it can be made in advance and
is ideal for any dinner party or family get-together.

**Serves
8**

**Sets in
4 hours**

✳

**Unsuitable
for freezing**

digestive biscuits

unsalted butter

Ingredients

250g (9oz) digestive biscuits

100g (3½oz) unsalted butter

4 sheets of gelatine, roughly cut up

finely grated zest and juice of 2 lemons

350g (12oz) cream cheese, at room
temperature

200g (7oz) caster sugar

300ml (10fl oz) double cream

lemon zest and juice

Special Equipment

23cm (9in) round springform cake tin

gelatine sheets

cream cheese

caster sugar

double cream

springform cake tin

Total time *35 minutes, plus minimum 4 hours chilling*

| **Prepare** | **Make** | **Set** |
| *5 minutes* | *30 minutes* | *4 hours or overnight* |

1 Line the tin with baking parchment. Place the biscuits in a freezer bag and crush to fine crumbs with a rolling pin. Melt the butter in a small saucepan. Stir the crumbs into the butter until well mixed, then firmly press the mix into the base of the tin.

Tip If the biscuit crumb mix looks a little dry and is not binding together enough, simply add a little more melted butter.

Crush the biscuits into fine, even-sized crumbs to ensure a firm base to the cheesecake

Slightly chill the gelatine once it has melted

2 Soak the gelatine in the lemon juice for 5 minutes. Melt it in a bowl set over a pan of simmering water. Remove from the heat and cool for 3–5 minutes. With an electric whisk, beat together the cream cheese, caster sugar, and lemon zest until very smooth, making sure there are no lumps.

Tip It is best to mix in softened cheese – simply remove from the fridge about an hour before using.

3 Clean the whisk attachments, then whisk the double cream in a bowl until it forms soft peaks. Whisk the gelatine into the cream cheese mixture until well mixed, then carefully fold the double cream into this mix using a figure-of-eight motion.

Careful! Fold the whipped cream in very gently, making sure you don't lose any volume.

It is easiest to fold the cream in gently using a spatula

4 Spoon the filling into the prepared cake tin, smoothing the surface so it is flat and even. Chill for 4 hours or overnight until firm. To release the cheesecake, unclip the sides of the tin and push the base up. Transfer it to a serving plate. Remove the metal base and parchment paper.

Tip Run a knife around the edge of the cheesecake before releasing it from the tin so it doesn't stick.

The perfect **Lemon Cheesecake**

Your lemon cheesecake should be set firm, with a light creamy texture and crisp biscuit base. If you like, decorate with strands of lemon zest using a zester.

Biscuit base is compact, even, and not too crumbly

Cream cheese topping is light and lump-free

Did anything go wrong?

The cheesecake is too soft. You may not have chilled it long enough to allow the gelatine to set. For best results, chill the cheesecake overnight.

The cheesecake has a lumpy texture. The cream cheese was not softened enough before you beat it in with the other ingredients. Next

time, make sure you take it out of the fridge at least an hour before using it.

The biscuit base is too crumbly. You may not have mixed in enough butter, which binds the crumbs together, or crushed the crumbs finely enough. Next time, crush the biscuits to a fine, uniform size and make sure to coat the crumbs completely with butter, adding more if needed.

Try more No-bake Cheesecake recipes ▶ ▶ ▶

Cherry Cheesecake

Serves 6 | **Sets in 2 hours** | **Unsuitable for freezing**

Ingredients

75g (2½oz) unsalted butter, plus extra for greasing

200g (7oz) digestive biscuits, finely crushed

2 x 250g tubs ricotta cheese, drained

75g (2½oz) golden caster sugar

finely grated zest and juice of 2 lemons

140ml (4½fl oz) double cream

6 sheets gelatine, cut into small pieces

400g can black cherries, or morello cherries in juice, drained and juice reserved

Special Equipment

20cm (8in) round springform cake tin

Grease and line the base of the springform cake tin with baking parchment.

MAKE THE CHEESECAKE

Melt the butter in a saucepan and stir in the crushed biscuits until well mixed. Spoon into the prepared tin, pressing down firmly, and transfer to the fridge.

Beat together the ricotta, sugar, and lemon zest until smooth.

Whisk the double cream in a separate bowl until it forms soft peaks. Stir the cream into the cheese mixture.

Meanwhile, place the lemon juice and gelatine in a small bowl and leave to soak for 5 minutes to soften the gelatine. Then heat gently over a saucepan of simmering water until the gelatine has dissolved, taking care not to boil the mixture as this can destroy the gelatine. Remove from the heat and cool slightly. Then slowly pour the

dissolved gelatine into the cheese mixture, stirring until well mixed. Spoon the cheesecake filling into the base, smoothing over the surface. Chill in the fridge for 2 hours or until set and firm.

DECORATE AND SERVE

Bring the cherry juice to a boil in a saucepan and simmer until reduced by three-quarters and syrupy. Leave to cool. To serve the cheesecake, carefully remove it from the tin and arrange on a serving plate.

Careful! It's best to run a palette knife around the edge of the cheesecake before removing it from the tin to prevent cracking.

Arrange the cherries on top, spoon over the sauce, and serve in slices.

Strawberry Cheesecake

Serves 8–10

Chill for 1 hour

Unsuitable for freezing

Ingredients

50g (1¾oz) unsalted butter

100g (3½oz) good-quality dark chocolate, broken into pieces

150g (5½oz) digestive biscuits, finely crushed

400g (14oz) mascarpone cheese, at room temperature

finely grated zest and juice of 2 limes

2–3 tbsp icing sugar, plus extra for dusting

225g (8oz) strawberries, hulled and halved

Special Equipment

20cm (8in) round springform cake tin

Line the base of the cake tin with baking parchment and set aside.

FORM THE BASE

Melt the butter and chocolate until smooth in a heatproof bowl set over a pan of simmering water (see p.96). Stir the melted mixture into the biscuit crumbs, then spoon into the tin, pressing the mixture down with a spoon until even. Chill in the fridge.

MAKE THE CHEESE FILLING

Beat the mascarpone in a bowl with the lime zest (saving a little for decoration), lime juice, and icing sugar to taste. Spoon over the biscuit base into the tin, smooth over the surface, and chill for 1 hour or until firm.

Remember As gelatine is not used to set this cheesecake, make sure it is chilled well until firm enough to cut into slices.

DECORATE AND SERVE

To serve, **carefully remove** the cheesecake from the tin and arrange on a serving plate. Place the halved strawberries around the edge, the reserved lime zest in the middle, and dust with icing sugar. Serve in slices.

Tip You can also use other biscuit flavours in place of digestives. For an extra chocolatey base, try chocolate chip cookies. Ginger nuts are also a good alternative.

How to use **Shop-bought Pastry**

As an alternative to making your own pastry, you can also use shop-bought pastry. Available in shortcrust and puff varieties, this pastry comes either in a block, ready for rolling out, or, for the ultimate convenience, ready-rolled in sheets. Think of it as a real time-saver, and not cheating – even experienced chefs use shop-bought puff pastry instead of making it from scratch.

Take the pastry out of its wrapping, cover with a clean tea towel to prevent it drying out, and leave at room temperature for 20 minutes before using

Puff pastry block

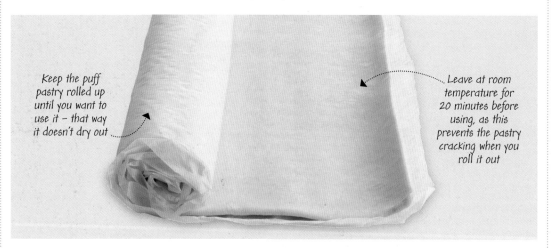

Keep the puff pastry rolled up until you want to use it – that way it doesn't dry out

Leave at room temperature for 20 minutes before using, as this prevents the pastry cracking when you roll it out

Ready-rolled puff pastry

Buying pastry

You can buy standard ready-made shortcrust and puff pastries as well as "all-butter" variations, which have a higher percentage of butter to give a superior, melt-in-the mouth taste. Both variations deliver consistent results on baking, but for extra flavour the all-butter pastry is recommended. All types of pastry, block or ready-rolled, are suitable for freezing.

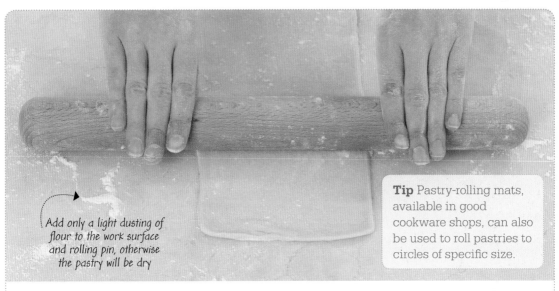

Add only a light dusting of flour to the work surface and rolling pin, otherwise the pastry will be dry

Tip Pastry-rolling mats, available in good cookware shops, can also be used to roll pastries to circles of specific size.

Rolling the pastry out

Place the unwrapped pastry on a lightly floured surface. With a lightly floured rolling pin, roll it out in long, even strokes away from you. Rotate it by 45° between strokes. For tarts and pies, the pastry is usually rolled out to 5mm (¼in) thick, but always refer to your recipe.

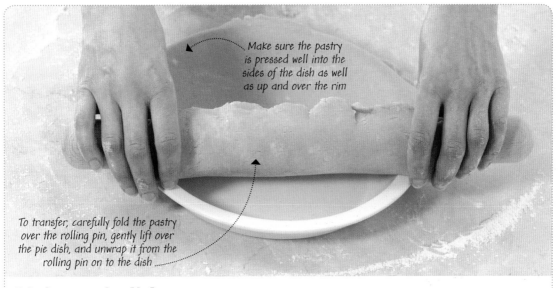

Make sure the pastry is pressed well into the sides of the dish as well as up and over the rim

To transfer, carefully fold the pastry over the rolling pin, gently lift over the pie dish, and unwrap it from the rolling pin on to the dish

Lining a pie dish

Roll out your pastry 5cm (2in) larger than your pie or tart dish. With a rolling pin, lift the pastry, drape it over the pie dish, and press into the base and sides. Trim off any excess pastry using a knife. Chill for 30 minutes to relax the pastry and so prevent shrinkage on baking.

Steak and Wild Mushroom Pie

Now you are armed with all the top tips for using shop-bought pastry, try this classic pie that's guaranteed to impress your guests. We'll show you how to make the perfect puff pastry lid – one that doesn't turn soggy during baking – along with how to create a decorative edge.

**Serves
4–6**

**Bakes in
25–35
minutes**

**Unsuitable
for
freezing**

Ingredients

1kg (2¼lb) braising steak, cut
into 2.5cm (1in) cubes

30g (1oz) plain flour, with a little salt
and pepper mixed in

500g (1lb 2oz) mixed fresh wild
mushrooms, wiped with a soft
clean cloth and sliced

4 shallots, finely chopped

900ml (1½ pints) beef stock,
plus extra if needed

salt and freshly ground black pepper

6 parsley sprigs, leaves finely chopped

500g (1lb 2oz) shop-bought puff pastry

1 egg, beaten, for egg wash

Special Equipment

2-litre (3½-pint) pie dish

braising steak

plain flour

**fresh wild
mushrooms**

shallots

beef stock

parsley sprigs

beaten egg

salt and pepper

puff pastry

pie dish

Total time *3 hours–3 hours 40 minutes*

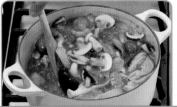

● **Prepare**
5 minutes

● **Make** *2½–3 hours, includes
cooking the stew*

● **Bake**
25–35 minutes

1 Preheat the oven to 180°C (350°F/Gas 4). Toss the steak in the flour. Place the steak, mushrooms, shallots, and stock in a casserole. Bring to a boil. Cover and cook in the oven for 2–2¼ hours until the meat is tender and the sauce thick. Adjust the seasoning, stir in the parsley, and transfer to the pie dish.

Why? Toss the steak in seasoned flour so the sauce thickens up.

The sauce should be rich and thick, else it will make the pastry soggy

To help bring the filling mixture to the boil quickly, add hot stock

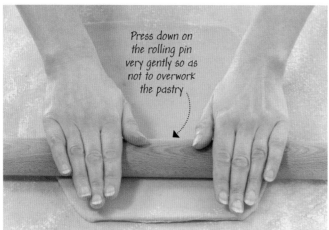

Press down on the rolling pin very gently so as not to overwork the pastry

2 Increase the oven temperature to 220°C (425°F/Gas 7). Roll out the pastry on a lightly floured surface until 5mm (¼in) thick and about 5cm (2in) bigger than the pie dish all around.

Remember To ensure even thickness, roll the pastry away from you using long strokes and rotating the pastry 45° after each roll.

3 Cut a thin strip from the rolled out pastry. Moisten the rim of the pie dish with cold water and place the pastry on to it. Brush the pastry rim with a little egg and top with the remaining dough, trimming off excess pastry.

Help! If your sauce is too runny, drain it off from the meat into a pan and boil rapidly until thickened and reduced slightly.

The strip of pastry around the rim sticks to the pastry lid and stops it from sliding into the pie

4 Firmly press the pastry lid onto the rim to seal. Flute the edge of the pastry by pressing a finger into the pastry and drawing the back of a knife inwards to make a short groove. Brush the lid with egg wash to give it a nice glaze when baked. Make a 1cm (½in) hole in the lid to allow the steam to escape while baking. Chill the pie for 15 minutes to relax the pastry and prevent it from shrinking, then bake for 25–35 minutes.

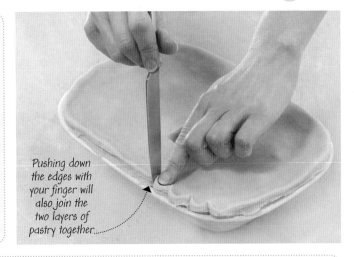

Pushing down the edges with your finger will also join the two layers of pastry together

The perfect **Steak and Wild Mushroom Pie**

Your finished pie should have a crisp, flakey, golden brown top and a filling that is deliciously moist.

Did anything go wrong?

The pastry has sunk. There may not have been enough filling to support the pastry lid, or there was too much liquid in the filling, or the pie dish was too large.

The pastry has not risen and is soggy. The oven must be preheated to 220°C (425°F/Gas 7) so the pastry cooks quickly before going soggy.

The pie filling has escaped from the pie dish and leaked everywhere. In this case, your pie dish may not have been large enough, causing the filling to boil over on baking.

The pastry has browned too much before cooking through and rising properly. Your rolled-out pastry may have been too thick. Next time, make sure it's no thicker than 5mm (¼in).

Pastry is golden brown, crisp, and cooked through

Filling is rich and thick, not runny

Try more Shop-bought Pastry bakes ▶ ▶ ▶

Fish and Leek Pie

Serves 4   **Bakes in 20–30 minutes**   **3 months, unbaked**

Ingredients

1 tbsp olive oil

1 onion, finely chopped

salt and freshly ground black pepper

4 leeks, finely sliced

1 tsp plain flour

150ml (5fl oz) cider

2 tbsp flat-leaf parsley, chopped

150ml (5fl oz) double cream

675g (1½lb) raw white fish, such as haddock, cod, or pollack, cut into chunks

300g (10oz) ready-made puff pastry

1 egg, beaten, for egg wash

Special Equipment

1.2-litre (2-pint) pie dish

Preheat the oven to 200°C (400°F/Gas 6).

MAKE THE FILLING

Heat the oil in a large frying pan, add the onion and salt, and fry gently for 4–5 minutes until soft and translucent. Add the leeks to the pan and cook gently for 8–10 minutes until softened. Stir in the flour, adding a little of the cider first to make a smooth paste, then gradually stir in the remaining cider to make a smooth sauce, and cook for 5–8 minutes or until thickened.

Careful! Make sure the sauce in the filling has thickened sufficiently before adding the fish, otherwise it can make the pastry soggy.

Stir the chopped parsley, cream, and fish into the leek mixture until well mixed. Season with salt and pepper. Spoon the filling into the pie dish.

TOP AND BAKE THE PIE

Roll out the pastry on a lightly floured surface until it is 5cm (2in) bigger than the pie dish. Cut a strip of pastry about 1cm (½in) wide all round to form the pastry rim and use this to edge the dish, fixing it with a little water.

Why? It's best to add a rim of pastry to the pie dish before topping with the lid to prevent the lid from sliding into the filling.

Brush the pastry rim with egg wash, then top with the pastry lid, trimming off any excess. Pinch the edges together to seal and cut 2 steam vents in the top of the pie with a knife. Brush the top of the pie liberally with the egg wash, then bake in the preheated oven for 20–30 minutes or until the pastry is well risen and golden brown. Serve hot.

Sausage Rolls

Makes 24

Bakes in 10–12 minutes

Up to 12 weeks, unbaked

Ingredients

250g (9oz) ready-made puff pastry

plain flour, for dusting

675g (1½lb) sausage meat

1 small onion, finely chopped

1 tbsp thyme leaves

1 tbsp finely grated lemon zest

1 tsp Dijon mustard

1 egg yolk

salt and freshly ground black pepper

1 egg, beaten, for glazing

PREPARE THE PASTRY

Cut the pastry in half lengthways, then on a lightly floured surface roll out each half to form a rectangle 30 x 15cm (12 x 6in). Cover with cling film and chill for 30 minutes. Preheat the oven to 200°C (400°F/Gas 6). Line a baking tray with baking parchment and chill.

Why? Chilling the pastry prevents it from shrinking too much while baking.

MAKE THE FILLING

In a bowl, combine the sausage meat, chopped onion, thyme, lemon zest, mustard, and egg yolk, and season to taste. Use your hands to give the ingredients a thorough mix, then divide into 2 equal amounts.

SHAPE AND BAKE THE ROLLS

Shape the sausage meat into 2 equal lengths, each long enough to be placed down the centre of the rolled-out puff pastry. Place the filling on the pastry, brush the edges of the pastry with

egg, and fold over to enclose the sausage filling. Press the edges together to seal, then cut each roll into 12 pieces. Arrange on the chilled baking tray, cut a slash in the top of each roll, and brush with beaten egg.

Why? Cutting a slash in the top of each roll will allow the steam to escape as it bakes, preventing the pastry from becoming soggy.

Bake the sausage rolls in the oven for 10–12 minutes or until the pastry is well risen and golden brown. Serve warm or transfer to a wire rack to cool completely.

How to make **Quick Breads**

Quick breads, as the name suggests, take no time at all to make. The dough for these breads requires very little kneading, and, as yeast is not used, the breads don't need to be left to rise or "prove". To make the breads rise, you replace the yeast with other raising agents, such as baking powder, bicarbonate of soda, or self-raising flour.

Buttermilk is found in the cream sections of supermarkets

Make a well in the centre of your ingredients, add the buttermilk, and gradually draw the dry ingredients into the buttermilk

Adding the buttermilk

Many quick breads use bicarbonate of soda as their raising agent, and for it to work well, you need to mix it with buttermilk. Buttermilk is a thick and creamy liquid, these days made by fermenting milk with lactic acid cultures. The buttermilk's acid reacts with the bicarbonate of soda to produce bubbles of carbon dioxide, making for light, well-risen breads.

It is normal for quick breads to have a slightly sticky dough

Make sure your surface is well dusted with flour

Bringing the dough together

Using lightly floured hands to prevent sticking, bring all the ingredients together until they form a rough dough, and shape into a ball.

The dough, at this stage, is likely to be a bit sticky. Don't worry about over-flouring the work surface, as this won't dry out your quick breads.

Push the dough forward with your knuckles, then fold it back on itself

Hold an end of the dough with one hand

Gently pat the dough into a round, smoothing over the surface

Kneading and shaping

Knead only to smooth out the dough, as the chemical raising agents will do most of the work in getting the bread to rise. As soon

as you have kneaded your dough, you need to shape it and bake it, as the raising agents will start working straightaway.

Soda Bread

Now you know how effortless it is to make quick
breads, try out this recipe for a quick and easy
soda bread that requires no kneading at all.

Makes 1 loaf

Bakes in 35–40 minutes

Unsuitable for freezing

Ingredients

500g (1lb 2oz) strong wholemeal bread flour, preferably stone-ground, plus extra for dusting

1½ tsp bicarbonate of soda

1½ tsp salt

500ml (16fl oz) buttermilk, plus extra if needed

unsalted butter, for greasing

strong wholemeal bread flour

bicarbonate of soda

buttermilk

salt

unsalted butter

Total time *50–55 minutes, plus cooling*

Prepare
5 minutes

Make
10 minutes

Bake
35–40 minutes

Work quickly to make a soft, slightly sticky, dough

1 Preheat the oven to 200°C (400°F/Gas 6). Sift together the flour, bicarbonate of soda, and salt into a bowl adding any leftover bran from the sieve. Make a well in the flour mix and pour buttermilk into the centre, drawing in the flour to make a soft dough.

Tip It's best to use your hands to mix the bread dough, as this will prevent overworking.

2 You should have a soft dough, but add a little extra buttermilk if it's too dry. Different flours will have slightly different absorbency levels, even between batches of the same flour. Turn the dough onto a floured surface and shape it into a round loaf.

Careful! If you overwork the dough, you will end up with a heavy loaf.

Shape just enough to get a smoothish dough, which may have some cracks

Cut a cross 1cm (½in) deep in the top of the loaf

3 Grease a baking sheet with the butter. Place the dough on it, shaping it and patting it down into a round approximately 5cm (2in) high. Using a sharp knife, cut a cross in the top of the loaf.

Why? Cutting a cross in the top of the dough makes it easier for the dough to expand, which helps the loaf rise up evenly on baking.

Tap the base of the loaf and, if cooked through, the bread should sound hollow

4 Bake the loaf for 35–40 minutes until it is well browned. Cool slightly on a wire rack – this allows the air to circulate freely around the loaf, preventing moisture being trapped underneath, which would make the bread soggy.

Tip This bread is best served warm, but will keep for 1–2 days in an airtight container.

The perfect **Soda Bread**

Your perfect soda bread will look golden brown, be well risen, and have a very light, almost cake-like texture.

The loaf has risen evenly

The "crumb" of the bread has a soft, light texture

The crust has a slight crunch to it without being too dry

Did anything go wrong?

The centre of the loaf feels damp. You haven't cooked the loaf for long enough. It should be completely dry in the centre.

The loaf has risen unevenly. You didn't sift the dry ingredients together properly resulting in uneven dispersal of the raising agent.

The soda bread is very dry. You have overbaked the loaf or kept it for too long – it really only keeps for a few days.

The outside crust of the soda bread is dry and hard. You may have baked the bread for too long, resulting in a hard crust. Next time, check the loaf after 35 minutes and if it sounds hollow when tapped on the base it is cooked through.

Try more Quick Bread recipes ▶ ▶ ▶

Pumpkin Bread

Makes   **Bakes in**   **Up to**
1 loaf   **50 minutes**   **8 weeks**

Ingredients

300g (10oz) plain flour, plus extra for dusting

100g (3½oz) wholemeal self-raising flour

1 tsp bicarbonate of soda

½ tsp fine salt

120g (4½oz) pumpkin or butternut squash, peeled, deseeded, and roughly grated

30g (1oz) pumpkin seeds

300ml (10fl oz) buttermilk

Preheat the oven to 220°C (425°F/Gas 7). Line a baking sheet with baking parchment.

MAKE THE DOUGH

Sift together the flours, bicarbonate of soda, and salt in a bowl. Add the grated pumpkin and seeds and mix well. Make a well in the centre and pour in the buttermilk.

Why? Combining bicarbonate of soda and buttermilk creates a reaction, producing carbon dioxide, which acts as the bread's raising agent.

Stir together until it combines to form a sticky dough. Turn the dough out onto a lightly floured surface and knead lightly for 2 minutes until it is smooth.

Help! If you find the dough is too sticky to knead, add a little extra flour.

SHAPE AND BAKE THE BREAD

Shape the dough into a 15cm (6in) round and place on the baking tray. Using a sharp knife, slash a cross in the top of the bread to help it rise when baking.

Bake in the preheated oven for 30 minutes until risen, then reduce the oven temperature to 200°C (400°F/Gas 6). Bake for a further 20 minutes or until cooked through. The base of the bread should sound hollow when tapped. Remove from the oven and cool slightly. Then transfer to a wire rack to cool for at least 20 minutes before serving. Cut the bread into slices or wedges and serve.

Tip This bread will keep for up to 3 days if well wrapped in paper.

Cornbread

Serves 8

Bakes in 20–25 minutes

Unsuitable for freezing

Ingredients

60g (2oz) unsalted butter, or bacon dripping
for extra flavour, melted and cooled, plus
extra for greasing

2 sweetcorn cobs, to yield about 200g (7oz) kernels

150g (5½oz) fine yellow cornmeal or polenta

125g (4½oz) strong white bread flour

50g (1¾oz) caster sugar

1 tbsp baking powder

1 tsp salt

2 eggs

250ml (8fl oz) milk

Special Equipment

23cm (9in) flameproof cast-iron frying pan, or
similar-sized loose-bottomed round cake tin

Preheat the oven to 220°C (425°F/Gas 7). Grease
the pan or tin with butter or dripping and preheat
the pan in the oven.

MAKE THE BATTER

Holding the corn cobs upright, carefully cut
the kernels from the cobs using a sharp knife.
Then scrape out any remaining pulp from the cobs
with the back of a knife and add to the kernels.

Tip If fresh corn on the cob is not available,
simply use 200g (7oz) drained canned sweetcorn
kernels instead.

Sift together the cornmeal or polenta, flour,
sugar, baking powder, and salt into a large bowl.
Stir in the corn. In a separate bowl, whisk together
the eggs, melted butter or bacon dripping, and

milk. Pour three-quarters of the milk mixture
into the flour mixture and stir, drawing in the
dry ingredients. Add the remaining milk mixture
and stir until just well mixed.

Careful! Do not overmix or the cornbread
may be tough.

BAKE THE BREAD

Using oven gloves, carefully take the preheated
pan out of the oven and pour in the batter. Don't
worry if it sizzles – this is normal. Quickly brush the
top with the butter or bacon dripping. Bake in the
oven for 20–25 minutes. When ready, the cornbread
should shrink away slightly from the sides of the
pan, and a skewer inserted into it should come out
clean. Remove from the oven and leave the bread to
cool slightly in its pan on a wire rack.

Cut the bread into wedges and serve while still
warm, as it does not keep very well.

2

Build On It

Now you can build on the techniques you've learnt with slightly more skilled recipes. Learn how to make classic creamed cakes, melt-in-the-mouth brownies, shortcrust pastry for savoury or sweet pies and tarts, as well as how to prepare the yeast and knead the dough for perfectly risen bread.

In this section, learn to bake:

Creamed Cakes
pp.82–95

Brownies
pp.96–105

Baked Cheesecake
pp.106–13

Shortcrust Tarts & Pies
pp.114–31

Yeast-risen Breads
pp.132–45

How to make **Creamed Cakes**

Some of the most traditional cakes, such as chocolate cake and Victoria sponge, are creamed cakes, which simply means you beat together the sugar and butter to a soft, creamy consistency before adding the other ingredients. Creaming is important because it gets air into the mixture to create perfectly light and fluffy cakes every time.

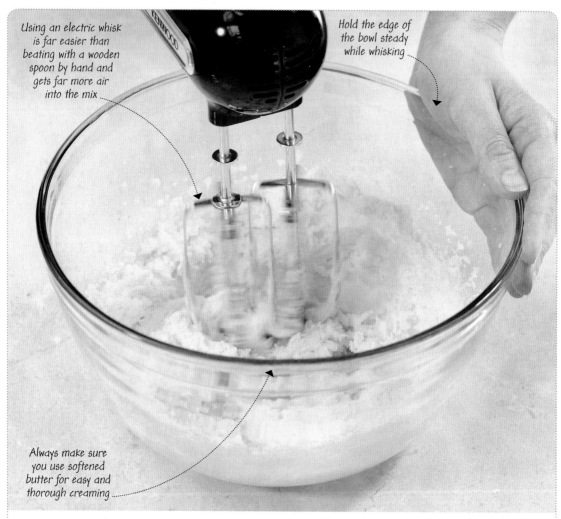

Using an electric whisk is far easier than beating with a wooden spoon by hand and gets far more air into the mix

Hold the edge of the bowl steady while whisking

Always make sure you use softened butter for easy and thorough creaming

Creaming

Whisk the butter and sugar together until the mixture is light and fluffy. Using an electric whisk is far easier than beating with a wooden spoon by hand and gets far more air into the mix. Creaming cuts the sugar crystals into the butter, creating air pockets, and so the more thoroughly you cream the mix, the lighter the cake will be.

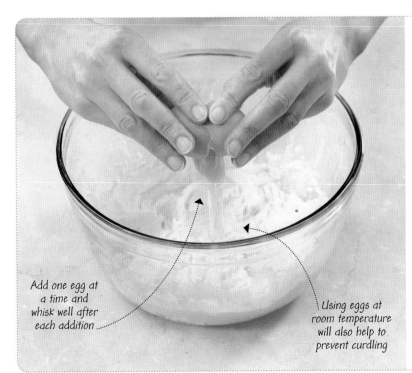

Adding the eggs

Eggs are added to the butter and sugar mix to bind all the ingredients together – they act as an emulsifier blending the ingredients for a smoother texture.

Take care to add the eggs gradually, as adding the eggs too quickly can curdle the mix and make it look like scrambled eggs. However, do not panic if that happens, simply add a tablespoon of flour with each addition of egg, then stir in the remaining flour.

Add one egg at a time and whisk well after each addition

Using eggs at room temperature will also help to prevent curdling

Sifting and folding

The dry ingredients are sifted together to help separate and aerate the flour particles, making them absorb liquids better and adding volume to the cake. To avoid knocking any of the air out, fold in the dry ingredients gently with a large metal spoon.

The science of Baking Cakes

Baking a cake harnesses precise chemical processes to transform a few simple ingredients into a mouth-watering slice of magic. Knowing the science involved in these transformations will help you to understand why certain ingredients and particular techniques create the best results.

1 Vigorously beating together fat and sugar – or "creaming" – creates an airy foam. As the ingredients are whisked, bubbles of air fix to the rough edges of the sugar crystals and are held in place by a film of fat.

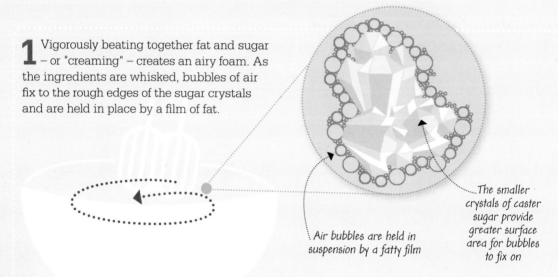

...The smaller crystals of caster sugar provide greater surface area for bubbles to fix on

Air bubbles are held in suspension by a fatty film

2 In the heat of the oven, as the air in the foam expands and the fat melts, the bubbles would burst. To prevent this, eggs are also beaten in, which, under heat, solidify around the bubbles to keep them intact.

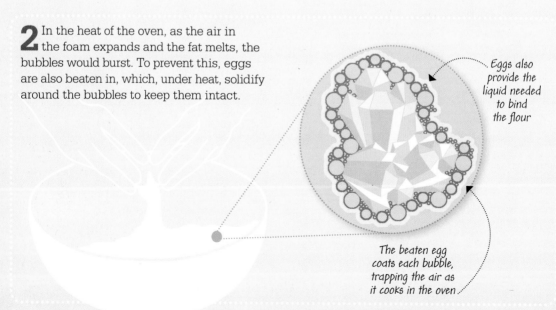

Eggs also provide the liquid needed to bind the flour

The beaten egg coats each bubble, trapping the air as it cooks in the oven

3 When mixed with a liquid, proteins in flour bind together to form a network of glutens, which soldify in the oven and provide structure to the cake. If too many glutens form, however, the cake will have a tough rather than soft and crumbly texture.

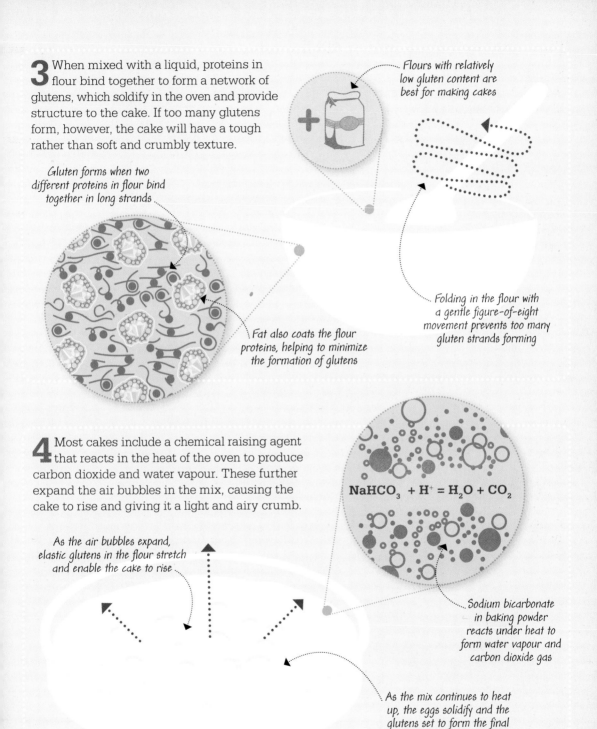

Flours with relatively low gluten content are best for making cakes

Gluten forms when two different proteins in flour bind together in long strands

Folding in the flour with a gentle figure-of-eight movement prevents too many gluten strands forming

Fat also coats the flour proteins, helping to minimize the formation of glutens

4 Most cakes include a chemical raising agent that reacts in the heat of the oven to produce carbon dioxide and water vapour. These further expand the air bubbles in the mix, causing the cake to rise and giving it a light and airy crumb.

$$NaHCO_3 + H^+ = H_2O + CO_2$$

As the air bubbles expand, elastic glutens in the flour stretch and enable the cake to rise

Sodium bicarbonate in baking powder reacts under heat to form water vapour and carbon dioxide gas

As the mix continues to heat up, the eggs solidify and the glutens set to form the final structure of the cake

Chocolate Cake

The secret to a good sponge is quite simply air and more
air, as this will guarantee a light and fluffy cake. Try this
classic chocolate cake, with a filling of buttercream and
a sprinkling of sugar, to prove to yourself just how
easy it is to make a creamed cake.

Serves 6–8

Bakes in 20–25 minutes

Up to 8 weeks, unfilled

Ingredients

175g (6oz) unsalted butter, softened, plus extra for greasing

175g (6oz) soft light brown sugar

3 eggs

125g (4½oz) self-raising flour

50g (1¾oz) cocoa powder

1 tsp baking powder

2 tbsp Greek yogurt or thick plain yogurt

For the filling

50g (1¾oz) unsalted butter, softened

75g (2½oz) icing sugar, plus extra for dusting

25g (scant 1oz) cocoa powder

a little milk, if needed

Special equipment

2 x 17cm (6¾in) round cake tins

unsalted butter

light brown sugar

eggs

self-raising flour

cocoa powder

baking powder

yogurt

icing sugar

round cake tins

Total time *55–60 minutes*

Prepare
5 minutes

Make
25 minutes

Bake
20–25 minutes

Decorate
5 minutes

1 Preheat the oven to 180°C (350°F/Gas 4). Grease the cake tins with butter. Line the base and sides with parchment. Set aside.

Tip For the sides, cut a length just longer than the tin's circumference. Make short 45° cuts with scissors along one of the long edges; this will then fold and sit neatly on the base. For the base, place a tin on baking parchment, draw a circle around the tin, and cut it out.

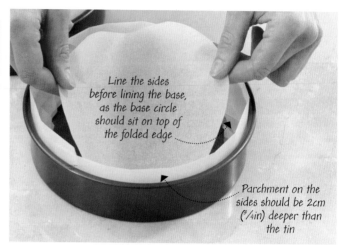

Line the sides before lining the base, as the base circle should sit on top of the folded edge

Parchment on the sides should be 2cm (³/₄in) deeper than the tin

Scrape down the sides of the bowl with a spatula to mix evenly

2 Place the softened butter and sugar in a large mixing bowl. Use an electric whisk to cream the two ingredients together until light and fluffy.

Remember You must cream the butter and sugar together for at least 2–3 minutes, otherwise your cake won't have a light texture. The more you beat at this stage, the more air you get into the mixture.

3 Add the eggs one at a time to the creamed mixture, beating well after each addition using an electric whisk. To begin with, the eggs will seem separate from the creamed mix, but on further blending, they will eventually combine and take on an "emulsified" or a well-blended appearance that is soft and creamy-looking.

The creamed mixture should look light and fluffy

4 Sift the flour, cocoa, and baking powder into a separate bowl. Then, with a metal spoon, gently fold into the mixture using a figure-of-eight motion. Also fold in the yogurt. The flour mixture must be gently folded in to avoid knocking any of the all-important air out of the mixture.

Tip Though not essential, for a really well aerated mix you can sift the dry ingredients a second time.

Hold the sieve as high as you dare

Gently tap the edge of the sieve

Spread the mixture right into the edges of the tin

5 Divide the mixture evenly between the 2 cake tins by placing alternate spoonfuls of the mix into each tin until you have the same amount in both the tins. Then smooth the mixture with a palette knife and bake for 20–25 minutes until well risen.

Tip Spread the mixture out so that there is a slight hollow in the centre, to prevent the cake from peaking in the centre.

6 The cakes are cooked when a skewer inserted into their centres comes out clean (see p.19, step 6). Leave to cool in their tins for 5 minutes, then remove from the tins and move the cakes to a wire rack to cool completely. Remove the baking parchment.

Help! Don't panic if the skewer comes out with some cake mixture on it. Simply bake the cakes for a few more minutes and then retest.

Peel off the baking parchment only after the cake cools down – any earlier and you may pull out some of the cake

7 To make the buttercream filling, mix together the butter, icing sugar, and cocoa by beating them together quite vigorously until smooth, soft, and thoroughly blended.

Help! If the buttercream is a little firm, add a drop of milk to the mixture and mix again until it is soft enough to spread.

After mixing, the buttercream should be soft enough to spread

Use a palette knife to spread the buttercream

8 Turn one of the sponges flat-side up and spread with the buttercream. Top with the other sponge, keeping the flat sides together. Transfer to a serving plate. Sift a little icing sugar evenly over the top by holding the sieve above the cake and tapping very gently, moving the sieve across the cake to ensure even coverage.

Tip This cake will keep for 2 days if stored in an airtight container.

The perfect **Chocolate Cake**

The perfect chocolate cake will be deliciously light and fluffy in texture with moist but well-risen layers when baked.

Top of the cake has a light dusting of icing sugar

Layer of buttercream is thick and spread out evenly

Sponge has a light and airy texture

Did anything go wrong?

The cake has sunk in the middle. You may have taken it out of the oven before it was cooked through. Next time, test your cake using a metal skewer and don't open the oven door too early to prevent the cake sinking.

The cake has a heavy texture. You may have added the eggs too quickly, which caused the mixture to curdle. A curdled cake mix will not bake so well because the mixture will be lumpy and separated, resulting in a coarser and heavier cake.

The cake seems too dry. You may have overcooked the cake or left it out for too long once cooled.

The cake has risen too much in the centre. You may have set the oven temperature to too high or added too much baking powder.

The cake hasn't risen very well. You may have either used insufficient baking powder or may have overbeaten the mixture, knocking the air out.

The sides of the cake are wet. You may not have removed the cake early enough from the tins to cool properly.

Try more Creamed Cake recipes ▶ ▶ ▶

Victoria Sponge Cake

Serves 6–8

Bakes in 20–25 minutes

Up to 4 weeks, unfilled

Ingredients

175g (6oz) unsalted butter, softened, plus extra for greasing

175g (6oz) caster sugar

3 eggs

1 tsp vanilla extract

175g (6oz) self-raising flour

1 tsp baking powder

For the filling

50g (1¾oz) unsalted butter, softened

100g (3½oz) icing sugar, plus extra for dusting

1 tsp vanilla extract

115g (4oz) good-quality seedless raspberry jam

Special Equipment

2 x 18cm (7in) round cake tins

Preheat the oven to 180°C (350°F/Gas 4). Grease the tins and line the base and sides with baking parchment. Set aside.

PREPARE THE MIXTURE

Cream together the butter and sugar using an electric whisk until light and fluffy. Add the eggs one at a time, beating well after each addition.

Careful! Always make sure the eggs are at room temperature to help prevent curdling.

Add the vanilla and blend into the creamed mixture. Then whisk for a further 2 minutes or until bubbles appear on the surface. Remove the whisks then sift together the flour and baking powder into the bowl. With a metal spoon, gently fold the flour into the mixture using a figure-of-eight motion.

BAKE THE CAKE

Divide the mixture between the tins and smooth the tops with a palette knife. Bake for 20–25 minutes until well risen. The cakes are cooked when a metal skewer inserted into their centres comes out clean.

Help! Don't panic if the skewer has cake mixture on it. Simply bake for a few more minutes and retest.

Leave the cakes to cool in the tins for 5 minutes, then remove the baking parchment and move the cakes to a wire rack to cool completely.

DECORATE AND SERVE

To make the buttercream filling, beat together the butter, icing sugar, and vanilla until smooth and very well mixed. Transfer one cake to a serving plate with flat side up and spread with the buttercream.

Tip If the buttercream is a little firm, add a drop of milk to slacken it slightly.

Spread the jam on top of the buttercream. Place the other cake on top of the filling, ensuring the flat sides are together. Sieve a generous layer of icing sugar over the cake and serve in slices.

Coffee and Walnut Cake

Serves 8

Bakes in 20–25 minutes

8 weeks, unfilled

Ingredients

275g (9½oz) unsalted butter, softened, plus extra for greasing

175g (6oz) soft light brown sugar

3 eggs

1 tsp vanilla extract

175g (6oz) self-raising flour

1 tsp baking powder

1 tbsp strong coffee powder mixed with 2 tbsp boiling water and cooled, or equivalent espresso

200g (7oz) icing sugar, sifted

9 walnut halves

Special Equipment

2 x 17cm (6¾in) round cake tins

Preheat the oven to 180°C (350°F/Gas 4). Grease and line the cake tins with baking parchment.

PREPARE THE MIXTURE

Place 175g (6oz) of the butter and sugar in a large bowl and, using an electric whisk, cream together for 2–3 minutes or until light and fluffy. Add the eggs to the creamed mixture one at a time, whisking well after each addition to prevent curdling.

Remember Using eggs at room temperature reduces the risk of curdling.

Stir in the vanilla. Sift the flour and baking powder, and fold into the creamed mixture until well mixed. Stir in half of the coffee mixture and make sure it is well incorporated.

BAKE THE CAKE

Divide the mixture between the 2 tins and smooth over their surfaces using a palette knife. Bake in the oven for 20–25 minutes or until well risen and a metal skewer comes out clean.

Remember Another way to check if the cakes are cooked is to see if they have begun to shrink away from the sides of their tins.

Leave the sponges in their tins for 5 minutes to cool slightly. Then remove from the tins and move to wire racks, discarding the baking parchment, to cool completely.

FILL, DECORATE, AND SERVE

To make the buttercream, place the remaining butter and icing sugar in a bowl and beat with an electric whisk until very smooth. Then beat in the remaining coffee mixture. Using a palette knife, evenly spread the flat side of one cake with half of the buttercream. Top with the other cake and spread with the remaining buttercream. Move to a serving plate, decorate with walnuts, slice, and serve.

Toffee Apple Cake

 Serves 8–10

 Bakes in 40–45 minutes

 Up to 4 weeks

Ingredients

200g (7oz) unsalted butter, softened, plus extra for greasing

50g (1¾oz) caster sugar

250g (9oz) apples, peeled, cored, and diced

150g (5½oz) soft light brown sugar

3 eggs

150g (5½oz) self-raising flour

1 heaped tsp baking powder

whipped cream, to serve (optional)

Special Equipment

23cm (9in) round springform cake tin

Preheat the oven to 180°C (350°F/Gas 4). Grease the cake tin and line its base with baking parchment.

PREPARE THE MIXTURE

In a frying pan, heat 50g (1¾oz) of the butter. Add the caster sugar and heat until melted and golden brown. Stir in the diced apple and cook for 7–8 minutes until they just start to soften and caramelize.

Careful! Constantly stir the apple mixture while cooking to prevent it from catching.

Place the remaining butter and sugar in a large bowl and, using an electric whisk, cream together for 2–3 minutes until light and fluffy. Add the eggs to the creamed mixture one at a time and whisk well after each addition to prevent curdling. Sift together the flour and baking powder, then gently fold into the creamed mixture until well mixed. Using a slotted spoon, remove the apple from the pan, reserving the syrup, and scatter the apple

over the base of the cake tin. Spoon the mixture on top, smooth over the surface with a palette knife, and place on a baking sheet to catch any drips.

BAKE AND FINISH

Bake in the preheated oven for 40–45 minutes or until well risen and a cake skewer comes out clean. Leave the cake to cool in the tin for at least 5 minutes, then carefully remove it from the tin, flipping it over so that the apples are at the top, and discarding the paper. Cool slightly on a wire rack. Gently heat the reserved apple syrup until warmed through and runny.

Why? You will need to reheat the reserved apple syrup as it may have thickened up too much to be of a pourable consistency.

Make holes over the surface of the cake, using a fine skewer, and transfer the cake to a serving plate. Pour the apple syrup over the top of the cake and allow time for it to soak into the holes. Serve the cake in slices while still warm, with whipped cream, if liked.

Cherry and Almond Cake

Serves 8–10 | **Bakes in 1½–1¾ hours** | **Up to 4 weeks**

Ingredients

150g (5½oz) unsalted butter, softened, plus extra for greasing

400g (14oz) cherries

150g (5½oz) caster sugar

2 large eggs

250g (9oz) self-raising flour, sifted

1 tsp baking powder

150g (5½oz) ground almonds

1 tsp vanilla extract

75ml (2½fl oz) whole milk

25g (scant 1oz) blanched almonds, halved

Special Equipment

20cm (8in) round springform cake tin

cherry pitter (optional)

Preheat the oven to 180°C (350°F/Gas 4). Grease the cake tin and line its base with baking parchment. Remove the cherry pips with a cherry pitter. Alternatively, take a cocktail stick and push it into the cherry where the stem was, and as soon as it hits the pip, twist the cocktail stick round and pull the cherry pip out.

PREPARE THE MIXTURE

Place the butter and sugar in a large bowl, and using an electric whisk, cream together for 2–3 minutes or until light and fluffy. Add the eggs to the creamed mixture, one at a time, with a tablespoon of flour and whisk well after each addition.

Why? Adding a tablespoon of flour with each egg prevents the cake mixture from curdling.

Mix in the remaining flour, baking powder, ground almonds, vanilla, and milk. Add half the cherries, then spoon the mixture into the tin, smoothing over the surface. Scatter the remaining cherries and almonds on the top.

BAKE THE CAKE

Bake in the preheated oven for 1½–1¾ hours or until golden brown and firm to the touch.

Careful! If the cake begins to brown too much, simply cover the top with foil.

Check if the cake is cooked through by inserting a metal skewer into the centre of the cake. If it comes out clean, the cake is cooked; if not, simply cook for a few minutes longer and retest. Remove the cake from the oven and leave to cool in the tin for at least 15 minutes. Then carefully remove the cake from the tin, discarding the paper, and transfer to a wire rack to cool completely. Slice and serve.

Tip This cake will keep for up to 2 days if stored in an airtight tin.

How to make **Brownies**

Brownies are a cross between a cake and a biscuit, and are typically made with melted chocolate and sometimes nuts for extra crunch. For the perfectly rich and chewy brownie, it's essential you melt the chocolate and butter slowly. And, whatever you do, don't overbake your brownies, as they'll lose their delicious, moist texture.

Careful! It is important that the base of the bowl sits above the water and doesn't touch it, or the chocolate will overheat and become grainy.

Don't forget to scrape the sides of the bowl

Melting the butter and chocolate

Begin by slowly melting the chocolate and butter in a bowl over a pan of simmering water. Never heat the chocolate in a pan over direct heat as this will cause the chocolate to overheat and turn grainy, or, worse still, "seize", which means it suddenly turns into an irreversible solid, grainy mass.

Also ensure the mixture doesn't come into contact with the water, as this could also cause the chocolate to seize. Stirring constantly with a wooden spoon keeps the temperature of the mixture even, prevents the chocolate from overheating, and helps to combine the butter and chocolate.

The mixture will thicken considerably on adding the eggs

Using eggs at room temperature will help prevent the mixture from curdling

Adding the eggs

Eggs form the next element in a brownie batter. Let the chocolate mixture cool before adding the beaten eggs, or the eggs will start cooking when you add them. To make a smooth batter, add the eggs slowly, a little at a time, stirring after each addition.

Sieving the cocoa and flour together helps to mix them

Gently tap the side of the sieve

The flour and cocoa particles attract air as they fall

Adding the flour

The final element of a basic brownie batter is flour, sometimes combined with cocoa. To add extra air, sift these dry ingredients into the chocolate mixture, and then gently fold them in with a spatula, using a figure-of-eight motion. This helps avoid knocking any air out, which would deflate the batter and result in heavy brownies.

Chocolate and Hazelnut Brownies

To achieve the perfect brownie, one that is rich, moist, and chewy, you need to follow just a few simple rules. Try this chocolate and hazelnut brownie recipe – great for an entry into the world of brownie-making.

Makes 24 | Bakes in 12–15 minutes | Unsuitable for freezing

Ingredients

100g (3½oz) hazelnuts

300g (10oz) good-quality dark chocolate, broken into pieces

175g (6oz) unsalted butter, diced

300g (10oz) caster sugar

4 large eggs, beaten

200g (7oz) plain flour

25g (1oz) cocoa powder, plus extra for dusting

Special Equipment

23 x 30cm (9 x 12in) rectangular brownie tin, or similar

hazelnuts

dark chocolate

unsalted butter

caster sugar

beaten eggs

plain flour

cocoa powder

rectangular brownie tin

Total time *47–50 minutes, plus cooling*

Prepare
5 minutes

Make
25 minutes

Bake
12–15 minutes

Decorate
5 minutes

1 Preheat the oven to 200°C (400°F/Gas 6). Scatter the hazelnuts on a baking sheet and toast in the oven for 5 minutes. Rub them in a tea towel to remove their skins, then transfer to a chopping board, and roughly chop using a large knife. Set aside.

Tip For an interesting texture, chop some of the hazelnuts into big chunks and some into small.

Toasting the hazelnuts makes it easier to rub their skins off, but be careful not to burn them

Make sure the bowl is supported by the pan and not sitting in the water, otherwise the chocolate will overheat

2 Place the chopped chocolate and butter in a heatproof bowl and sit it over a pan of simmering water. Heat until melted and smooth, stirring occasionally. Cool slightly for 5 minutes, then stir in the sugar until well mixed.

Careful! Do not let the water heat above simmering point, as this could cause the chocolate to become grainy.

3 Add the eggs a little at a time, mixing well between each addition, until you have a smooth mixture.

Careful! Before adding the eggs, make sure they are at room temperature and the chocolate mixture has cooled down sufficiently, or you'll end up with scrambled eggs.

Use a wooden spoon to beat the mixture quite vigorously

4 Sift the flour and cocoa into the mixture, holding the sieve at a height to incorporate as much air as possible. Gently fold in the flour and cocoa until everything is fully mixed in. Add the chopped toasted hazelnuts into the batter and fold in until the nuts are mixed and evenly distributed.

Tip For best results, sift the flour and cocoa together twice, using a separate bowl, before folding in.

Tip in the hazelnuts when no traces of flour or cocoa are left

For ease of spreading, use a spatula

5 Line the brownie tin with baking parchment, then add the batter. Using a spatula, spread the mixture out evenly so that it fills the corners properly, and smooth over the top.

Tip Leave a little extra parchment paper round the sides of the tin for easy removal.

Make diagonal cuts into the corners of the parchment so it fits easily into the corners of the tin

Try to get the surface as smooth and even as possible

6 Cook the brownies in the oven for 12–15 minutes. Test if they have cooked on top by pressing the middle with two fingers: it should feel firm to the touch. Test that the centres are still chewy by inserting a skewer.

Remember Brownies should be chewy, and it's best to underbake them as they firm up on cooling, so do check them after 10–12 minutes of baking.

...The brownies are done if a skewer inserted comes out coated with a little batter, but not a lot of very wet batter

7 Leave the brownies to cool down completely in the tin. This helps to maintain their soft, chewy centre and, being very fragile at this stage, they could break if removed from the tin any sooner. When cool, carefully lift them from the tin and place them on a chopping board.

Tip Use the edges of the baking parchment paper to help lift the brownies out of the tin.

8 Put freshly boiled water in a shallow bowl. Using a knife, cut the brownies into 24 squares, dipping the knife in the hot water as you go. Place 1 tablespoon of cocoa in a sieve, hold it over the brownies, and gently tap with your hand to give the brownies a light coating of cocoa. Then serve.

Why? Wetting the knife helps you to cut the brownies cleanly without the mix sticking to the knife.

You can cut the brownies into larger squares, if preferred

The perfect **Chocolate and Hazelnut Brownies**

Your cooked brownies should be firm around the edge, but their centres should be deliciously soft and chewy.

A flat surface

Cut into even squares

A generous layer of cocoa on top

An even distribution of chopped nuts

Did anything go wrong?

The brownie batter looks lumpy and curdled. You may have added the eggs before the chocolate mixture had cooled down enough or used eggs that were straight from the fridge and too cold.

The brownies are far too wet. You may not have baked them for long enough or you used a tin that was smaller than the one suggested. If the tin is a bit smaller, the brownie mix will be more compacted. Increase the cooking time by a minute or two, checking frequently to see if it is cooked.

The brownies have collapsed on removing them from the tin. You may not have cooled the brownies completely before removing them

from the tin. Remember, they firm up a lot when completely cooled.

The brownies are very dry. You may have baked them for too long. It's important to get the texture right, so if in doubt, underbake them.

The brownies are tough. The batter may have been overbeaten after adding the eggs and flour. Gently fold these in so as not to knock the air out.

The brownies are heavy. The batter may have been overbeaten after folding in the flour and cocoa.

Some of the brownies have more nuts than the others. You may not have stirred the nuts into the batter evenly.

Try more Brownie recipes ▶ ▶ ▶

Sour Cherry and Chocolate Brownies

Makes 16

Bakes in 20–25 minutes

Unsuitable for freezing

Ingredients

150g (5½oz) unsalted butter, diced plus extra for greasing

150g (5½oz) good-quality dark chocolate, broken into pieces

250g (9oz) light brown muscovado sugar

3 eggs, lightly beaten

1 tsp vanilla extract

150g (5½oz) self-raising flour

100g (3½oz) dried sour cherries

100g (3½oz) dark chocolate chunks

Special Equipment

20 x 25cm (8 x 10in) brownie tin, or similar-sized deep baking tray

Preheat the oven to 180°C (350°F/Gas 4). Grease the tin and line with baking parchment.

PREPARE THE MIXTURE

Place the butter and chocolate in a heatproof bowl and sit the bowl over a saucepan of simmering water, stirring occasionally, until melted and smooth (see p.96). Remove from the heat and stir in the sugar, then cool slightly for 5 minutes. Mix the eggs and vanilla extract into the cooled chocolate mixture.

Careful! Let your chocolate mixture cool slightly before adding the eggs, otherwise they will begin to cook.

Sift the flour into a bowl, then pour the chocolate mixture onto the flour and stir until just well combined, taking care not to overwork the mixture. Then fold in the cherries and chocolate chunks.

BAKE THE BROWNIES

Pour the mixture into the prepared tin and spread it out to the corners, smoothing the mixture over so it's even. Bake for 20–25 minutes. The brownie is ready when the edges are firm but the middle is still soft. Leave to cool in the tin, as it will be very fragile, before carefully turning out and cutting into 16 squares.

Remember Brownies are supposed to be slightly soft in the centre after baking so, unlike other cakes, if testing with a skewer, it should not come out clean.

Tip These brownies will keep very well for up to 3 days if stored in an airtight container.

White Chocolate and Macadamia Blondies

Makes 24

Bakes in 20 minutes

Unsuitable for freezing

Ingredients

300g (10oz) white chocolate, broken into pieces

175g (6oz) unsalted butter, diced

300g (10oz) caster sugar

4 large eggs

225g (8oz) plain flour

100g (3½oz) macadamia nuts, roughly chopped

Special Equipment

20 x 25cm (8 x 10in) brownie tin, or similar-sized deep baking tray

Preheat the oven to 200°C (400°F/Gas 6). Grease the tin and line with baking parchment.

PREPARE THE MIXTURE

Place the chocolate and butter in a heatproof bowl and sit the bowl over a saucepan of simmering water, stirring occasionally, until melted and smooth (see p.96). Do not let the bowl touch the water.

Careful! The mixture must be melted over just simmering, and not boiling, water, otherwise the chocolate will overheat and become grainy.

Remove the bowl from the heat, stir in the sugar, and cool for 10 minutes before adding the eggs. Beat the eggs into the melted mixture one at a time, making sure each one is well mixed in before adding the next. Sift in the flour, add the nuts, and stir together until just mixed.

BAKE THE BLONDIES

Pour the mixture into the prepared tin and gently spread it out to the corners. Bake for 20 minutes or until just firm to the touch on top but still soft underneath.

Remember The blondies will firm up further on cooling.

Remove from the oven and leave to cool completely in the tin, as the blondie will be very fragile. Then cut into 24 squares or 12 rectangles.

Tip These blondies will keep very well for up to 5 days if stored in an airtight container.

How to make **Baked Cheesecake**

Baked cheesecakes typically have a crushed biscuit base and a creamy, velvety smooth topping. Unlike the cheesecakes that are set with gelatine, they rely on the eggs in the mix to set the filling during baking. Sometimes flour is included in the cream cheese mix to bind the ingredients, as well as cream and different cream cheeses, such as ricotta or mascarpone.

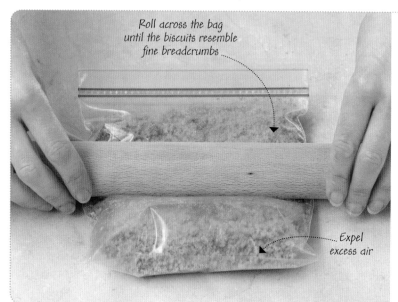

Roll across the bag until the biscuits resemble fine breadcrumbs

Expel excess air

Crushing the biscuits

To make the base, first pop the biscuits in a freezer bag. Seal and roll a rolling pin across the bag until the crumbs are of a uniform size. A fine crumb will hold the cheesecake's base together whereas a rough crumb will crumble and fall apart more easily. You can also crush the biscuits in a food processor.

Making the biscuit base

Mixing butter into the biscuit crumbs binds the crumbs together to give the cheesecake a firm base. To form the base, press the mixture firmly into the cake tin, or other dish, using the back of a spoon.

Make sure the biscuit mixture completely covers the base of the tin, otherwise the filling will escape

Blending the filling

Blend the filling ingredients thoroughly so you don't get a lumpy mix. It also helps if your cream cheese and eggs are at room temperature before you beat them together. The eggs act as an emulsifier, binding together the ingredients that normally wouldn't mix easily. If using a food processor, stop as soon as the mix is fully blended, so you don't get too many air bubbles in the mix, which could lead to the surface cracking during baking.

You can blend the filling ingredients by hand, but it's quicker and more thorough in a food processor

The cheesecake is ready if it feels slightly wobbly in the centre

Why? Cheesecakes are often baked in a bath of boiling water. This insulates the pan from direct heat and maintains a low cooking temperature, allowing the cheesecake to cook slowly and evenly.

Testing for a set

The key to a perfect cheesecake is knowing when to stop baking. If cooked perfectly, the edges will be set but the centre still wobbly as the filling will firm up further as it cools. If you overbake the cheesecake it will become tough and rubbery in texture.

Blueberry Ripple Cheesecake

The ripple effect of this cheesecake looks impressive and is guaranteed to deliver the "wow" factor when entertaining friends or family. However, don't be put off by this, as it's surprisingly simple to achieve.

Serves 8 | **Bakes in 40 minutes, plus cooling** | **Unsuitable for freezing**

unsalted butter   digestive biscuits   blueberries

Ingredients

50g (1¾oz) unsalted butter, plus
   extra for greasing

125g (4½oz) digestive biscuits

150g (5½oz) blueberries

150g (5½oz) caster sugar, plus
   3 tbsp extra

400g (14oz) cream cheese,
   at room temperature

250g (9oz) mascarpone,
   at room temperature

2 large eggs, plus 1 large egg yolk,
   at room temperature

½ tsp vanilla extract

2 tbsp plain flour, sifted

caster sugar   cream cheese   mascarpone

eggs

egg yolk

vanilla extract   plain flour

Special Equipment

20cm (8in) deep springform cake tin

food processor with blade attachment

springform cake tin   food processor

Total time *1 hour 5 minutes, plus at least 5 hours cooling and chilling*

Prep
5 minutes

Make
20 minutes

Bake
40 minutes

1 Preheat the oven to 180°C (350°F/Gas 4) and grease the cake tin well with butter. Crush the biscuits in a freezer bag using a rolling pin. Melt the butter in a pan and stir in the biscuit crumbs. Spoon the mixture into the tin, pressing it down firmly and evenly.

Tip Heat the butter over a low heat to avoid burning it, as this would give a burnt flavour and an unwanted brown colour.

...To avoid a crumbly base, ensure the crumbs are well coated in butter

2 Process the blueberries and 3 tbsp of sugar in a food processor until smooth. Sieve the purée to remove the skins, place it in a pan, and boil for 3–5 minutes to achieve a jam-like consistency, so that it can be marbled into the cheese mix without sinking. Once thickened, set aside.

Why? Boiling the purée vigorously helps concentrate the flavour and also gives it a jam-like consistency.

3 In a food processor, blend the remaining sugar, cream cheese, mascarpone, eggs, vanilla extract, and flour. Stop processing once thoroughly blended and smooth, or you'll add air bubbles, which cause the cheesecake to crack on baking. Spoon the mix into the tin and smooth the surface with a spatula or palette knife.

Remember Ensure your cheeses are softened before blending.

Check the mixture is properly mixed with no traces of egg, cream cheese, or flour.

Don't forget to scrape down the sides of the processor bowl

Place dollops of the blueberry mix evenly over the filling, then break them up with a skewer, making swirls

4 Drizzle on the blueberry mix and swirl it using a skewer. Wrap the base and sides of the tin with foil and place in a roasting tin half-filled with boiling water. Bake for 40 minutes until set but wobbly in the centre. Turn off the oven. Leave for 1 hour, then remove from the oven and cool completely on a wire rack. Transfer to a refrigerator to chill for at least 4 hours or overnight.

The perfect **Blueberry Ripple Cheesecake**

For a blueberry compote to serve alongside, gently heat 100g (3½oz) blueberries with 1 tablespoon of caster sugar and a squeeze of lemon juice in a small pan until the sugar dissolves and the berries start to release their juices.

Did anything go wrong?

The cheesecake mixture is lumpy. You may not have mixed the ingredients well or they were probably not at room temperature before mixing.

The cheesecake has sunk in the centre. Did you let it cool slowly in the turned-off oven before chilling?

The cheesecake split open when I removed it from the tin. You need to grease the tin well before adding the filling and run a palette knife around the edges to free the cheesecake before serving.

The cheesecake has a rubbery texture. You may have overbaked the cheesecake. Next time check earlier to see if it has baked. Don't be put off by a wobbly centre – it should be just firm to the touch in the centre with a bit of wobble. If there is no wobble, it is overbaked, and if a finger pressed in the middle leaves a dent, it is underbaked.

The surface is smooth and not cracked

The cheese filling is smooth and set, and firmer around the edge

The base is crunchy

Try more Baked Cheesecake recipes ▶ ▶ ▶

Chocolate Marble Cheesecake

Serves 8–10   **Bakes in 60 minutes, plus cooling**   **Unsuitable for freezing**

Ingredients

75g (2½oz) unsalted butter, melted, plus extra for greasing

150g (5½oz) digestive biscuits, finely crushed

150g (5½oz) good-quality dark chocolate, broken into pieces

500g (1lb 2oz) cream cheese, softened

150g (5½oz) caster sugar

1 tsp vanilla extract

2 eggs

Special Equipment

20cm (8in) round springform cake tin

Grease the cake tin with butter and chill.

MAKE THE BASE AND FILLING

Add the melted butter to the biscuit crumbs, stirring until well mixed, then spoon into the tin and press the mixture over the base and up the sides of the tin. Chill for 30–60 minutes or until firm. Preheat the oven to 180°C (350°F/Gas 4). Place the chocolate in a heatproof bowl set over a pan of simmering water and heat until melted and smooth (see p.96). Remove from the heat and allow to cool slightly.

Careful! Make sure the water is just simmering as too much heat will cause the chocolate to turn grainy.

Whisk the cream cheese in a bowl until smooth. Add the sugar and vanilla and beat well. Add the eggs, one at a time, beating well after each addition. Pour half of this mixture into the lined tin. Stir the melted and cooled chocolate into the remaining half of the cheesecake mixture. Spoon

a ring of the chocolate filling over the plain filling and, using a metal skewer, swirl the fillings together to create an attractive marbled effect.

BAKE AND SERVE

Bake the cheesecake for 50–60 minutes, at which point most of the cheesecake is firm, but the centre will still wobble slightly. Turn off the oven and leave the cheesecake inside to cool for 1½ hours.

Why? Cooling down the cheesecake in the turned-off oven helps prevent it from cracking.

Remove the cooled cheesecake from the oven and chill in a fridge for at least 4 hours, or ideally overnight. To serve, run a knife around the side of the tin to loosen it, remove from the tin, and arrange on a serving plate. Serve in slices.

Tip The cheesecake can be made up to 3 days ahead and stored wrapped in cling film in the fridge until needed.

Ginger Cheesecake

Serves 8–10 | **Bakes in 60 minutes, plus cooling** | **Unsuitable for freezing**

Ingredients

75g (2½oz) unsalted butter, melted, plus extra for greasing

150g (5½oz) digestive biscuits, finely crushed

500g (1lb 2oz) cream cheese, softened

125g (4½oz) stem ginger in syrup, chopped, plus 3 tbsp syrup

finely grated zest of 1 lemon

2 tsp lemon juice

250ml (8fl oz) soured cream

150g (5½oz) granulated sugar

1 tsp vanilla extract

4 eggs

150ml (5fl oz) double cream, to top (optional)

Special Equipment

20cm (8in) round springform cake tin

Grease the cake tin with butter and chill.

MAKE THE BASE AND FILLING

Add the melted butter to the biscuit crumbs, stirring until well mixed, then spoon into the tin and press the mixture over the base and up the sides of the tin. Chill for 30–60 minutes or until firm. Preheat the oven to 180°C (350°F/Gas 4). Beat the cream cheese in a bowl until smooth.

Careful! Always ensure your cream cheese is very smooth before beating in the other ingredients, otherwise you will have a lumpy filling.

Add the chopped ginger (reserving 2 tablespoons to decorate), ginger syrup, lemon zest and juice, soured cream, sugar, and vanilla. Beat until

smooth. Add the eggs one at a time, beating well after each addition. Pour the filling onto the base and shake slightly to level the surface.

BAKE AND DECORATE

Place the tin on a baking tray and bake in the oven for 50–60 minutes. The cheesecake is cooked when most of it is firm, but the centre will still wobble slightly. Turn off the oven and leave the cheesecake inside to cool for 1½ hours.

Why? Cooling down the cheesecake in the turned-off oven helps prevent it from cracking.

Chill in the fridge for 4 hours, or ideally overnight. If using double cream, whip it until it forms soft peaks. To serve, run a knife around the side of the tin to loosen it. Remove from the tin and arrange on a serving plate. Swirl or smooth the cream over the top of the cheesecake and decorate with a scattering of the reserved chopped stem ginger. Serve in slices.

Tip The cheesecake can be made up to 3 days in advance and stored wrapped in cling film in the fridge.

How to make **Shortcrust Pastry**

Shortcrust pastry is one of the easiest pastries to make. It is used to line savoury and sweet tarts and pies, and it doesn't puff up on baking. For light and meltingly tender pastry, the key is to keep everything cold, including your hands, and not to overwork the dough.

Lift the flour with pieces of the butter, keeping the palms facing up to aerate the mix, and rub between your thumb and fingers to form fine crumbs

Hands are cool

Butter is cool, straight from the fridge

Sieve the flour first to add extra air and lightness to the pastry

Tip To save time, you could pulse the flour and butter together in a food processor until the mixture resembles fine breadcrumbs.

Rubbing in

This technique coats the flour with the butter, reducing gluten formation when mixing the dough. This gives a "shortness" or tenderness to the pastry. It is important to use only your fingertips when rubbing the butter into the flour as this minimizes contact with body heat, which would melt the butter and make the pastry heavy and greasy.

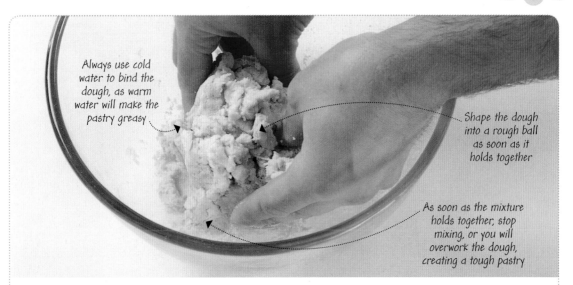

Always use cold water to bind the dough, as warm water will make the pastry greasy

Shape the dough into a rough ball as soon as it holds together

As soon as the mixture holds together, stop mixing, or you will overwork the dough, creating a tough pastry

Forming the dough

Begin by mixing in enough cold water to bind the dough together. Use a round-bladed knife until the mixture begins to come together to form a soft, but not sticky, dough. Too much water will cause the pastry to steam on baking, which will make it flimsy and shrink back. Sometimes egg yolk is also added, which may be enough to bind the dough together without any additional, or very little, water. Then form into a rough ball with your hands.

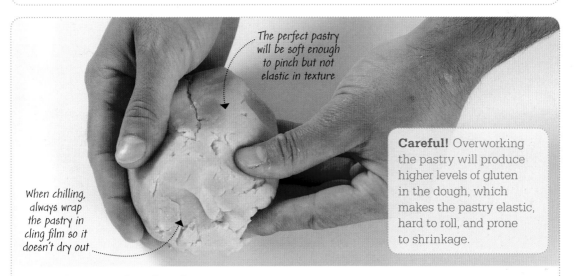

The perfect pastry will be soft enough to pinch but not elastic in texture

When chilling, always wrap the pastry in cling film so it doesn't dry out

Careful! Overworking the pastry will produce higher levels of gluten in the dough, which makes the pastry elastic, hard to roll, and prone to shrinkage.

Shaping and relaxing

Shortcrust pastry must be chilled in a fridge for at least 30 minutes to relax the gluten in the dough and to prevent it from shrinking back as it bakes. Shape it into a ball without overworking the dough, which could make the pastry greasy and tough.

The science of Making Pastry

Pastry dough should remain fundamentally weak: just strong enough
to be rolled and shaped, but still brittle so that once baked it will break
apart easily into tender, melt-in-the-mouth flakes. To achieve this, the
gluten proteins in flour, which bind together to provide structure, must
be gently coaxed together and steps taken to minimize their strength.

1 Rubbing together the flour and fat is not
just a means of mixing ingredients. As you
rub, you are coating a proportion of the flour
particles with fat, and this will inhibit the
formation of glutens in the dough.

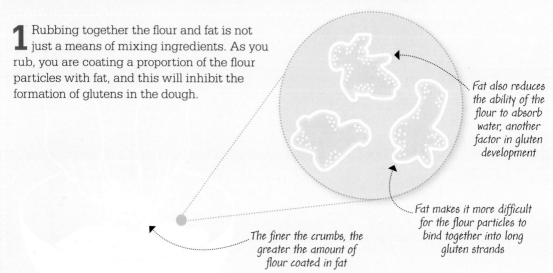

*Fat also reduces
the ability of the
flour to absorb
water, another
factor in gluten
development*

*Fat makes it more difficult
for the flour particles to
bind together into long
gluten strands*

*The finer the crumbs, the
greater the amount of
flour coated in fat*

2 Water must be mixed into flour before
gluten can start to form. Less water means
less gluten and this is why only a small amount
of water is added to pastry dough, a little at
a time, and enough for the mixture to just
hold together in a ball.

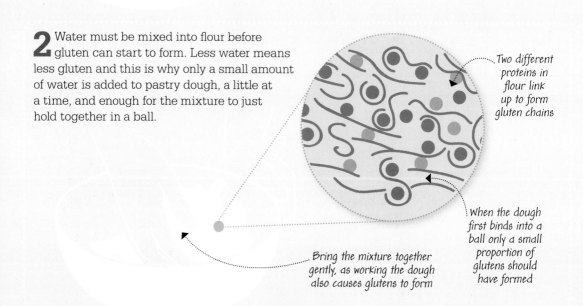

*Two different
proteins in
flour link
up to form
gluten chains*

*When the dough
first binds into a
ball only a small
proportion of
glutens should
have formed*

*Bring the mixture together
gently, as working the dough
also causes glutens to form*

3 Pastry dough should only be lightly kneaded, if at all. Before it is flexible enough to roll out, more glutens are required to give the dough elasticity, but the baker must leave time to do most of the work.

The dough is left to "rest" for at least 30 minutes, wrapped in cling film so it doesn't dry out

Water moves throughout the resting dough until it is evenly distributed

More gluten strands form as flour in the drier pockets of dough absorbs water

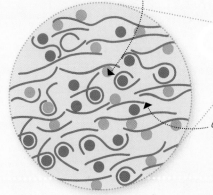

Gluten has time to relax so that when the dough is rolled out it doesn't spring back and won't shrink in the oven

Resting the dough in the fridge stops the fat melting, which can make the pastry greasy

4 The fat content in the dough plays another crucial role in achieving a light, flaky texture to the cooked pastry. In the heat of the oven, the relatively large pieces of fat melt and leave behind pockets of air.

Different sized chunks of fat leave irregular spaces between layers of pastry

Avoid stretching the pastry as you line the tin, since this will cause the glutens to tighten more in the heat of the oven and cause shrinkage

Some of the air pockets left by the melted fat are expanded by vaporising water in the dough

In the high heat of the oven the gluten and starch quickly set to hold the shape of the pastry as the fat melts

Swiss Chard and Gruyère Tart

Perfect for a picnic or a lazy summer lunch, this tart is
equally delicious served hot or cold. To create a light and
crispy pastry, keep the dough cool, work quickly, and use
the lightest of touches. Don't forget that you can always
use spinach if you can't find Swiss chard.

Serves 6–8

Bakes in 30–40 minutes

Up to 8 weeks

Ingredients

For the pastry

75g (2½oz) unsalted butter, chilled and diced

150g (5½oz) plain flour, plus extra for dusting

1 egg yolk

For the filling

1 tbsp olive oil

1 onion, finely chopped

sea salt

2 garlic cloves, finely chopped

a few sprigs of fresh rosemary, leaves picked and finely chopped

250g (9oz) Swiss chard or spinach, stalks removed and leaves roughly chopped

125g (4½oz) Gruyère cheese, grated

125g (4½oz) feta cheese, cubed

freshly ground black pepper

2 eggs, lightly beaten

200ml (7fl oz) double cream

Special Equipment

23cm (9in) loose-bottomed tart tin

baking beans

unsalted butter

plain flour

olive oil

egg yolk

beaten eggs

onion

sea salt

garlic

rosemary

double cream

Gruyère cheese

feta cheese

Swiss chard or spinach

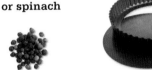
black pepper

loose-bottomed tart tin

baking beans

Total time *2 hours 20 minutes–2 hours 35 minutes, including 1 hour chilling time*

Prepare
5 minutes

Make *45–50 minutes + 1 hour chilling*

Bake
30–40 minutes

1 To make the pastry, rub the butter and flour together until the mixture forms fine crumbs. Beat the egg yolk with 1 tbsp of cold water and add it to the crumb mixture.

Remember Make sure your hands are cold before rubbing in the butter. Run them under cold water for a minute, drying them afterwards. Or, press your hands against an ice cooler block.

Use your fingertips to rub the flour and butter together to keep the mix as cool as possible

Quickly shape your dough into a very rough ball to prevent overworking it

2 Using a round-bladed knife to minimize contact with your hands, stir the egg mixture into the crumbs until you can bring the mixture together to form a soft dough. Quickly shape the dough into a ball, drawing in the crumbs from the sides of the bowl too.

Careful! Add only enough egg mixture to form a soft but not sticky dough. It doesn't matter if you don't use all the egg.

3 Wrap the ball of dough in cling film and chill in the fridge for 1 hour. Preheat the oven to 180°C (350°F/Gas 4). Gently roll out the dough, making sure you don't press down too hard, until approximately 3mm (⅛in) thick.

Why? Chilling the dough will help to relax it and prevent it from shrinking during baking.

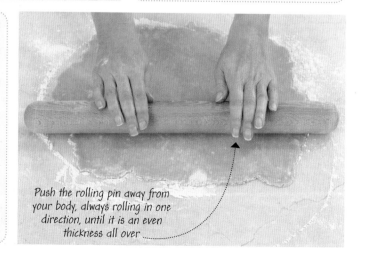

Push the rolling pin away from your body, always rolling in one direction, until it is an even thickness all over

4 Carefully fold the pastry over the rolling pin, then gently lift the pastry on to your tart tin, and unwrap it over the tin. Line the tin by pushing the pastry in with your fingers and leaving at least 2cm (¾in) of the pastry hanging over the edges.

Why? Leave an overhang of pastry in case the pastry shrinks slightly on baking. You can trim off the excess pastry once baked.

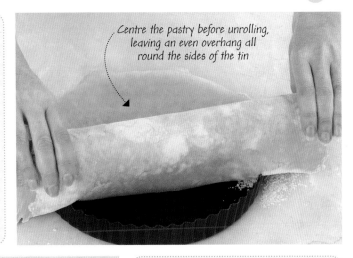

Centre the pastry before unrolling, leaving an even overhang all round the sides of the tin

Lightly prick all over the base, just so you leave an indentation with a fork but don't go all the way through

You can use ordinary dried beans or uncooked rice instead of baking beans

5 Lightly prick the base of the pastry with a fork and place the tin on a baking tray. Line the tin with baking parchment and fill it with baking beans.

Why? Pricking the pastry base with a fork prevents it from bubbling up as it cooks. Baking beans weigh the pastry down, giving it an even base and preventing it from rising on baking.

6 Bake the tart case for 20–25 minutes, remove the paper and beans, and bake for a further 5 minutes to crisp up the base. Trim the edges with a knife to remove the excess pastry.

Why? Cooking the pastry first without the filling, called "baking blind", keeps the base crisp. Cooking the base with the filling would take too long, causing the filling to overcook or even burn.

Trim away from the tin to avoid getting crumbs in the base

7 Pour the oil into a frying pan. Fry the onion with a pinch of salt over a low heat for 2–3 minutes. Add the garlic and rosemary and cook for a few seconds. Stir constantly to avoid burning. Add the Swiss chard and cook for about 5 minutes until it just wilts.

Careful! Don't overcook the Swiss chard, as it will release too much of its water and make the tart's filling very wet.

Stir to prevent burning and stop cooking as soon as the chard starts to wilt

8 Spoon the chard filling into the pastry case and spread it evenly over the base of the tart. Scatter grated Gruyère all over and then dot with the feta cheese over the top. Season well.

Tip If preferred, you could crumble the feta cheese over the filling rather than adding it as cubes.

9 Beat the remaining eggs and double cream together using a fork, and carefully pour over the tart, so it doesn't just settle in the middle of the filling. Let it seep into the case, then bake for 30–40 minutes or until golden and just set. Leave to cool slightly before releasing from the tin.

Careful! To avoid spillage, place the tart on the baking sheet before you pour the egg mixture in.

The perfect **Swiss Chard and Gruyère Tart**

Your finished tart should have a crisp pastry case and a firm, creamy filling.

Top is lightly caramelized

The Swiss chard is evenly dispersed with the feta cheese

The egg cream mix has set, and the filling isn't wet

Thin, crisp, golden pastry

Did anything go wrong?

The pastry case has shrunk. You may have added too much liquid to the dough or you didn't chill the pastry for long enough before baking. It needs to chill for at least 1 hour in the fridge.

The filling is very wet and not set. You may have overcooked the chard. If the chard gives off liquid, drain it off before you add it to the pastry case.

The filling has started to seep out of the base. When pricking the uncooked pastry base, you may have pricked all the way through to the metal tin. Make sure you only lightly prick the pastry.

The filling is dry and very rubbery. You may have overcooked the tart. As some ovens are naturally hotter than others, check the tart after 30 minutes to see if it is ready. You know the tart is ready when the middle of the filling has just set.

Try more Shortcrust Tarts ▶ ▶ ▶

Quiche Lorraine

Serves 4–6

Bakes in 25–30 minutes

Up to 8 weeks, baked

Ingredients

150g (5½oz) plain flour, plus extra for dusting

75g (2½oz) unsalted butter, diced

1 egg yolk

200g (7oz) bacon lardons

1 onion, finely chopped

75g (2½oz) Gruyère cheese, grated

4 large eggs, lightly beaten

150ml (5fl oz) double cream

150ml (5fl oz) milk

freshly ground black pepper

Special Equipment

23 x 4cm (9 x 1½in) round, deep tart tin

baking beans or dried beans

MAKE THE PASTRY

Sift the flour into a bowl, add the diced butter, and, using your fingertips, rub the butter in until the mixture looks like breadcrumbs. Then add the egg yolk and 3–4 tablespoons cold water or enough to make a smooth, but not sticky, dough. Wrap in cling film and chill for 30 minutes. Preheat the oven to 190°C (375°F/Gas 5).

Roll the pastry out on a lightly floured surface and use it to line the tin, trimming off any excess. Prick the base gently with a fork, then line with baking parchment and baking beans. Bake blind for 12 minutes. Remove the paper and beans, and bake for another 10 minutes or until golden brown and cooked through.

Why? Baking your pastry case blind ensures the pastry case will remain crisp once it has been baked with the filling in it.

MAKE THE FILLING AND BAKE

Heat a frying pan and dry fry the bacon lardons for 3–5 minutes; they will release their fat. Add the onion and fry for a further 2–3 minutes until softened slightly. Place the cooked pastry case on a baking tray before adding the bacon and onion filling. Scatter the bacon and onion into the pastry case with the cheese.

Remember Scatter the bacon and onion evenly into the pastry case otherwise you will end up with an unevenly filled quiche.

Whisk together the eggs, cream, milk, and pepper to taste, then pour into the case. Bake in the oven for 25–30 minutes or until just set and golden brown. Remove from the oven and leave to cool very slightly before cutting into slices.

Onion Tart

Serves 6

Bakes in 15–20 minutes

Up to 8 weeks, baked

Ingredients

150g (5½oz) plain flour

75g (2½oz) unsalted butter, diced

1 egg yolk

1 tbsp olive oil

4 onions, sliced

1 tbsp plain flour

300ml (10fl oz) milk

2 tsp mild paprika

salt and freshly ground black pepper

Special Equipment

23cm (9in) loose-bottomed tart tin

baking beans or dried beans

Why? Adding a small amount of milk to the flour allows you to make a smooth paste, which then makes it easier to mix in the remaining milk without any lumps forming.

Stir in 1 teaspoon of the paprika, season well, and set aside.

MAKE THE PASTRY AND FILLING

Sift the flour into a bowl, add the diced butter, and, using your fingertips, rub the butter in until the mixture looks like breadcrumbs. Add the egg yolk and 3–4 tablespoons cold water or enough to make a smooth, but not sticky, dough. Wrap in cling film and chill for 30 minutes. Preheat the oven to 200°C (400°F/Gas 6).

Heat the oil in a non-stick frying pan. Add the onions and sweat very gently for 10–15 minutes, stirring constantly, until the onions are soft and translucent.

Careful! Cook the onions over a low heat, as you want them softened but not coloured.

Remove from the heat and stir in the flour. Add a little of the milk, and stir well. Return to the heat, add the rest of the milk, and heat gently, stirring constantly until the mixture thickens.

MAKE THE PASTRY CASE AND BAKE

On a lightly floured surface, roll the pastry out and use it to line the tin, trimming off any excess. Prick the base gently with a fork, then line with baking parchment and baking beans. Bake the pastry case blind for 12 minutes. Remove paper and beans and bake for a further 10 minutes or until golden in colour and cooked through. Remove from the oven and place on a baking tray before filling with the onion mixture. Reduce the oven temperature to 180°C (350°F/Gas 4). Carefully spoon the filling into the pastry case, sprinkle over the remaining paprika, and bake in the oven for 15–20 minutes or until just set and golden brown. Cool slightly before cutting into slices and serving.

Remember As this tart is not made with eggs, the filling will not set firm and will have more of an open texture.

How to make **Sweet Shortcrust Pastry**

Sweet shortcrust pastry is crispier and more delicate than standard
shortcrust pastry because it is made with extra butter and more
egg yolk. The pastry is sweetened with sugar and has a delicious,
crumbly texture after it is baked. This does not make the dough harder
to work with, provided it is properly chilled before you roll it out.

Egg yolks give richness and colour to the mix

Sweetening and enriching the dough

Add sugar to your rubbed in butter and flour
mix to sweeten the dough. Then add beaten
egg yolks and a little cold water, if needed.

The fat in the yolk, with the butter, acts as a
shortening agent, preventing the gluten in the
dough linking, to keep the pastry crumbly.

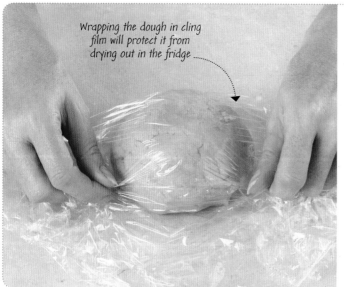

Wrapping the dough in cling film will protect it from drying out in the fridge

Relaxing the dough

It is especially important to chill
sweet shortcrust pastry as it is
fragile and tricky to roll out if not
chilled enough. Chilling allows
the dough's gluten to relax and
prevents it from shrinking during
baking. If the dough does begin
to fall apart on rolling out, don't
worry – carefully drape it over the
rolling pin, transfer to the tin and
press into the base, pinching
together any cracks and
smoothing over the surface so
there are no gaps in the dough.

How to make **Crème Pâtissière**

Crème pâtissière is a classic pastry cream, a little like a very thick custard, which is used in fresh fruit tarts and other desserts. It is thickened with cornflour and, unlike custard, it won't separate when cooked, but it requires careful attention and constant whisking to ensure it remains smooth and thickened enough without any lumps forming.

... Whisk all the time as you pour in the milk

Making the crème base

As your crème pâtissière must be thick and very creamy, you must whisk your ingredients for the crème base until very smooth. You first make a batter-like base from flour, eggs, and sugar. Whisk until very smooth before pouring in the heated milk, whisking constantly.

Custard is very thick when ready ....

Tip To cool, spoon the crème into a bowl and top with a round of greaseproof paper to prevent a skin from forming.

Cooking the crème

Gently cook the crème over a low heat, for approximately 3 minutes, whisking constantly with a balloon whisk, until it changes from a thin to a very thick, smooth consistency. To test if the crème is ready, remove the whisk – if it leaves a thick trail that won't disappear, the creme is ready. Continuous whisking will also prevent the crème from curdling and sticking to the pan. Make sure you cook the crème well in advance as it needs through chilling before use.

Strawberry Tart

**Serves
6–8**

**Bakes in
25 minutes**

**Up to 12
weeks,
unfilled**

Ingredients

100g (3½oz) unsalted butter, chilled and diced

150g (5½oz) plain flour, plus extra for dusting

150g (5½oz) caster sugar

1 egg yolk, plus 2 whole eggs

1½ tsp vanilla extract

6 tbsp redcurrant jelly, for glazing

50g (1¾oz) cornflour

400ml (14fl oz) whole milk

300g (10oz) strawberries, hulled and thickly sliced

Special Equipment

23cm (9in) loose-bottomed tart tin

baking beans or dried beans

MAKE AND BAKE THE PASTRY

Rub the butter into the sifted flour until the
mixture resembles breadcrumbs. Stir in 50g (1¾oz)
sugar. Beat together the egg yolk and ½ tsp vanilla,
and mix into the flour mixture with a little water,
if needed, to form a soft dough. Wrap in cling film
and chill for 1 hour. Preheat the oven to 180°C
(350°F/Gas 4). On a lightly floured surface, roll
the pastry out to 3mm (⅛in) thickness. Line the
tin with the pastry, trimming off any excess.
Prick the base gently with a fork, line with baking
parchment and baking beans, and place on a
baking tray. Bake blind for 20 minutes, remove
the paper and beans, and bake again for 5 minutes.
Melt the jelly with 1 tbsp water, then brush a little
over the pastry case and cool.

Why? Brushing with melted redcurrant jelly
creates a sweet glaze that will help to stop the
pastry getting soggy when the filling is added.

MAKE THE FILLING

To make the crème pâtissière, beat the
remaining sugar, cornflour, eggs, and 1 tsp vanilla
together in a bowl. Heat the milk in a saucepan to
just below the boil. Pour into the egg mixture,
whisking constantly. Return the crème to the pan
and cook over a medium heat, whisking constantly
for 4–5 minutes or until thickened. Reduce the heat
and cook for 2–3 minutes over a low heat. Transfer
to a bowl, cover with cling film, and cool completely.

ASSEMBLE AND SERVE

Beat the cooled crème pâtissière until smooth,
then spread it over the pastry case to give an even
layer. Top with the strawberries, arranging them in
circles starting from the outside edge and working
into the centre. Heat the jelly mixture again until
runny then brush over the strawberries and leave
to set. Carefully remove the tart from the tin and
place on a serving plate.

Remember To save time, the crème pâtissière
can be made a day ahead and cooled overnight.
Just make sure you give it a good beating to soften
it slightly before spreading it into the pastry case.

Raspberry Tart with Chocolate Cream

Serves
6–8

Bakes in
20–25
minutes

Up to 12
weeks,
unfilled

Ingredients

125g (4½oz) plain flour, plus extra for dusting

20g (¾oz) cocoa powder

100g (3½oz) unsalted butter, chilled and diced

150g (5½oz) caster sugar

1 egg yolk, plus 2 whole eggs

1½ tsp vanilla extract

50g (1¾oz) cornflour

450ml (15fl oz) whole milk

175g (6oz) good-quality dark chocolate,
   broken into pieces

400g (14oz) raspberries

icing sugar, for dusting

Special Equipment

23cm (9in) loose-bottomed tart tin

baking beans or dried beans

MAKE AND BAKE THE PASTRY

Sift the flour and cocoa into a bowl. Add the butter and rub in until the mixture looks like breadcrumbs. Stir in 50g (1¾oz) of the sugar. Beat together the egg yolk and ½ tsp vanilla, add to the flour mixture, and form a soft dough; add water, if a little dry. Wrap in cling film and chill for 1 hour. Preheat the oven to 180°C (350°F/Gas 4). On a lightly floured surface, roll the pastry out to 3mm (⅛in) thickness and line the tin with it, trimming off any excess. Prick the base gently with a fork, line with baking parchment and baking beans, and place on a baking tray. Bake for 20 minutes, remove the paper and beans, and bake for a further 5 minutes until cooked through. Remove from the oven and leave to cool.

MAKE THE FILLING

Beat the remaining sugar, cornflour, eggs, and 1 tsp vanilla in a bowl. Bring the milk and 100g (3½oz) chocolate to just below the boil, whisking all the time until chocolate has melted. Pour the hot milk onto the egg mixture, whisking nonstop. Then return the chocolate crème to the pan and cook over a medium heat, for 4–5 minutes or until thickened, whisking all the time. Reduce the heat to low and cook for a further 2–3 minutes, whisking constantly. Transfer the chocolate crème to a bowl, cover with cling film to prevent a skin forming, and cool completely.

ASSEMBLE AND SERVE

Melt the remaining chocolate in a heatproof bowl set over a pan of simmering water. Brush over the cooked pastry base and leave to set. Remove the pastry case from the tin and arrange it on a serving plate. Beat the chilled chocolate crème until smooth, then spoon into the case. Top with the raspberries and lightly dust with icing sugar using a fine sieve.

Tip You can prepare the pastry and crème pâtissière a day earlier, but the prepared tart is best eaten the same day.

How to make **Double-crust Sweet Pies**

Double-crust sweet pies are deep-filled fruit pies that are lined with a sweet shortcrust pastry base and topped with a lid, giving you the "double crust". Unlike tarts, you don't blind bake the base of a double-crust pie since it is first cooked at a higher temperature to firm up the pastry base and lid. You then reduce the heat and bake it for longer to finish the cooking process. A double-crust pie base, however, will never be as crispy or dry as a tart's base.

Gently press the pastry into the base and sides of the dish, smoothing out any bubbles in the pastry

Trim excess pastry with a sharp knife for a neat edge

Lining the pie dish

On a lightly floured surface, roll out half of the pastry to a circle about 5cm (2in) wider than the pie dish, so you have enough pastry to line the dish. Drape the pastry over the dish, then press it into the base and sides, trimming off any excess at the very edge of the dish at a slight angle. This helps reduce shrinkage as it bakes.

Egg wash creates a seal

Use a rolling pin to transfer and unwrap the pastry

Filling and topping the pie

Spoon the filling into the dish and, using a pastry brush, brush the pastry rim with beaten egg, known as egg wash. Roll out the remaining dough and use it to top the pie. Press the edges together to seal, then flute the edge with the back of a knife (see p.69).

Apple Pie

Serves 6–8

Bakes in 50–55 minutes

Unsuitable for freezing

Ingredients

350g (12oz) plain flour, plus extra

½ tsp salt

150g (5½oz) lard or white vegetable fat, diced, plus extra for greasing

100g (3½oz) caster sugar, plus extra

1kg (2¼lb) tart apples, peeled, cored and cut into medium slices

juice of 1 lemon

½ tsp ground cinnamon, or to taste

¼ tsp grated nutmeg, or to taste

1 egg, beaten, to brush

1 tbsp milk, for glazing

Grease a 23cm (9in) round, shallow pie dish.

MAKE THE PASTRY

Sift the flour and salt into a bowl, add the diced fat, and rub in until the mixture resembles breadcrumbs. Stir in 2 tablespoons sugar, then add 6 tablespoons cold water, or just enough, to bring the mixture together to form a soft dough. Shape into a ball, wrap in cling film, and chill for 30 minutes.

ASSEMBLE THE PIE

Roll out half of the pastry on a lightly floured surface. Use the pastry to line the dish, gently pressing into the base and up the sides. Trim off any excess pastry and chill for 15 minutes. Place apple slices in a bowl with the lemon juice and toss until well coated. Sprinkle in 2 tablespoons flour, 100g (3½oz) sugar, cinnamon, and nutmeg, and stir until well mixed.

Why? Adding flour to the apple mix slightly thickens up the juices in the filling during baking.

Spoon the apple mix into the pie dish, filling more in the centre so that you create a slight mound. Brush the pastry on the edge of the dish with the egg wash and roll out the remaining pastry to cover the pie completely. Lift the pastry onto the pie dish and trim off any excess. Press the edges together to seal, crimping the edges as you go. Cut an X in the middle of the crust and pull back the point of each triangle to reveal the filling. If you like, decorate the pie with strips of pastry trimmings, using a little water to secure. Brush the top with the milk, sprinkle over a little sugar, and chill for 30 minutes. Preheat the oven to 220°C (425°F/Gas 7).

BAKE AND SERVE

Bake the pie for 20 minutes, then reduce the temperature to 180°C (350°F/Gas 4), and bake for a further 30–35 minutes or until crisp and golden brown. Cover loosely with foil if the pie starts browning too much. Serve warm.

Rhubarb and Strawberry variations Mix together the following for the filling: 1kg (2¼lb) sliced rhubarb, finely grated zest of 1 orange, 250g (9oz) caster sugar, and ¼ tsp salt. Stir in 375g (13oz) hulled and halved strawberries. Spoon into the pastry-lined pie dish. Dot 15g (½oz) diced butter over the filling, then continue as in the recipe.

How to make **Yeast-risen Bread**

Yeast-risen breads need flour with a higher gluten content to produce a good bread structure and rely on yeast to make them rise. To create a well-risen loaf, you must rehydrate the yeast ("proof it"), knead the dough to stretch and develop the gluten within it, leave it to rise, then "knock back" the air from the dough, and proof it for one final rise before baking.

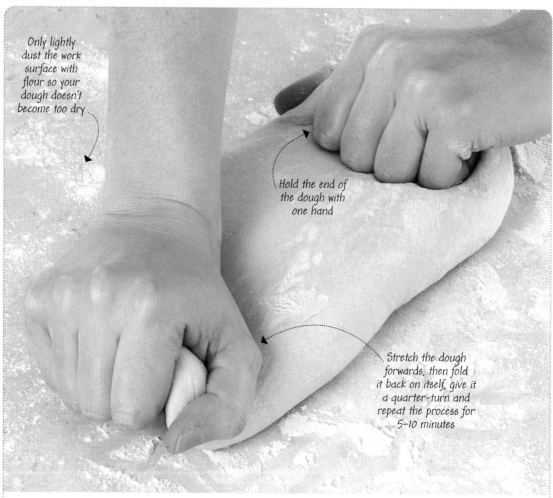

Only lightly dust the work surface with flour so your dough doesn't become too dry

Hold the end of the dough with one hand

Stretch the dough forwards, then fold it back on itself, give it a quarter-turn and repeat the process for 5–10 minutes

Kneading the dough

Kneading stretches the dough and develops the gluten in the flour, helping the loaf rise. Keep turning the dough by a quarter-turn each time you push it forward and fold it back on itself. This will ensure the gluten is evenly formed and the yeast well-distributed. If you don't knead your dough well enough, you'll end up with a poorly risen loaf. Your dough is ready when it is smooth and "springs back" when pressed with a finger.

Cling film creates a warm, moist environment that allows the dough to rise and prevents it from drying out

It's best to cover the bowl with cling film but a clean tea towel will do

Always put the dough in a lightly oiled bowl to prevent it from sticking

Leaving the dough to rise

Leave your dough to rise in a warm place for an hour or so until it doubles in size. Leaving your dough in a cool environment will slow down the rising process considerably. Rising allows the ingredients to work together to produce carbon dioxide, while the developing gluten enables the dough to stretch, which traps carbon dioxide in the mix. On baking, the gas evaporates from the dough to leave a well-risen bread with a light texture.

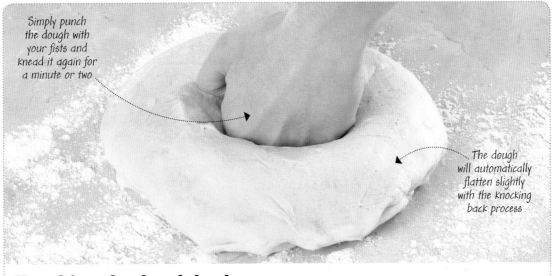

Simply punch the dough with your fists and knead it again for a minute or two

The dough will automatically flatten slightly with the knocking back process

Knocking the dough back

You need to knock back the newly risen dough to remove any excess carbon dioxide and knead it again briefly to redistribute the yeast within the dough. You then need to shape the dough and leave it to proof for one final rise before baking.

The science of Baking Bread

The chemical process going on inside fermenting bread dough is in essence the same as for brewing beer. In both instances, yeast is encouraged to feed on the sugars in processed grain to produce carbon dioxide gas and alcohol. Key to bread making is to trap this gas inside the dough and use it to create the wonderfully light texture of bread.

1 Only three ingredients are needed for bread: flour, yeast, and water. Yeast is a microscopic living organism, a kind of fungi, with an ability to ferment the sugars in flour.

Water hotter than 45°C (113°F) will inhibit yeast activity; above 60°C (140°F) and the yeast will die

Water is absorbed by the starch content in flour and enzymes then begin to break down the starch into sugars for the yeast to feed on

Recipes call for lukewarm water since this helps create the optimum temperature in the dough for yeast to thrive: 25–30°C (77–86°F)

2 Unlike cake mix and pastry, bread dough must be worked on vigorously – "kneaded" – to encourage the formation of glutens that will give the dough its vital elasticity.

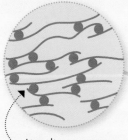

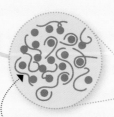

Kneading also helps create a smooth, even texture and distributes the yeast throughout the dough

Kneading encourages more proteins to combine into gluten, which link up into a stretchy, elastic structure

Gluten is made from two different proteins in flour that start to combine with each other as soon as water is added

The dough is ready when you can stretch it without tearing

3 The yeast is then left to do its business of converting sugar into carbon dioxide gas and alcohol. The gas stretches the elastic dough but cannot escape and so forms lots of small pockets in the dough.

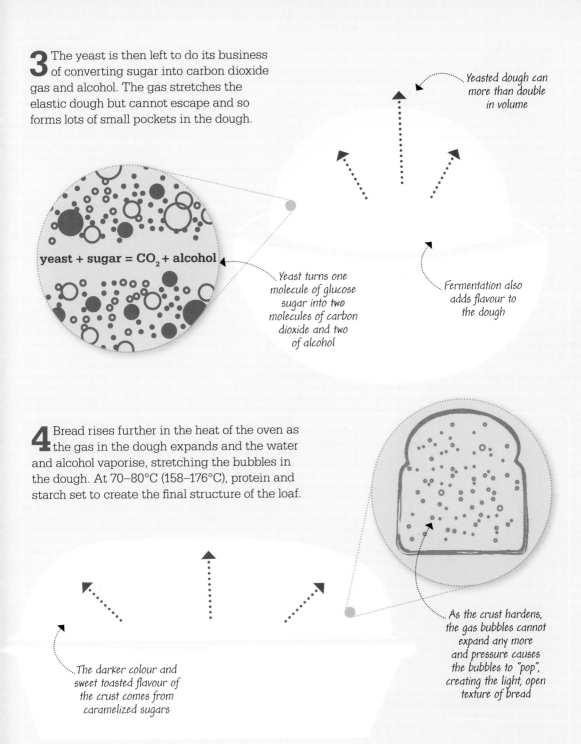

Yeasted dough can more than double in volume

yeast + sugar = CO₂ + alcohol

Yeast turns one molecule of glucose sugar into two molecules of carbon dioxide and two of alcohol

Fermentation also adds flavour to the dough

4 Bread rises further in the heat of the oven as the gas in the dough expands and the water and alcohol vaporise, stretching the bubbles in the dough. At 70–80°C (158–176°C), protein and starch set to create the final structure of the loaf.

As the crust hardens, the gas bubbles cannot expand any more and pressure causes the bubbles to "pop", creating the light, open texture of bread

The darker colour and sweet toasted flavour of the crust comes from caramelized sugars

Rosemary Focaccia

Focaccia is an Italian bread made with yeast-risen dough enriched and flavoured with olive oil, and topped with herbs. Focaccia dough is well-tempered and easy to make, so it's a perfect recipe for a novice.

Serves 6–8

Bakes in 15–20 minutes

Unsuitable for freezing

Ingredients

1 tbsp dried yeast

425g (15oz) strong white bread flour, plus extra for dusting

2 tsp salt

leaves from 5–7 sprigs of rosemary, two-thirds finely chopped

90ml (3fl oz) olive oil, plus extra for greasing

¼ tsp freshly ground black pepper

sea salt flakes

Special Equipment

38 x 23cm (15 x 9in) deep baking tray or Swiss-roll tin

dried yeast

strong white bread flour

salt and sea salt flakes

olive oil

rosemary

black pepper

deep baking tray or Swiss-roll tin

Total time *2 hours 20 minutes–3 hours 10 minutes, including 1½–2¼ hours rising time*

Prepare
5 minutes

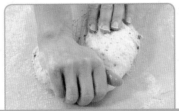

Make
30 minutes + rising time

Bake
15–20 minutes

1 Proof the yeast by sprinkling it over 4 tablespoons lukewarm water and letting it stand for 5 minutes. Sift the flour and salt into a large bowl, making a well in the centre. Add the chopped rosemary, yeast mix, 4 tablespoons olive oil, and 250ml (8fl oz) lukewarm water. Gradually draw in the flour and work into a smooth dough.

Careful! Use lukewarm water to soak the yeast; hot water will kill it.

After proofing, the yeast mixture will look frothy and bubbly

The dough will have a smooth, elastic texture when ready and will spring back when pressed with a finger

2 Turn the dough onto a floured surface and knead for 5–7 minutes. Shape it into a round, which aids rising, then place in a lightly oiled bowl, cover, and leave to rise for 1–1½ hours until doubled in size. Turn it out onto a work surface again and knock out the air by punching the dough with your fists. Knead very briefly, then cover again, and leave to rest for a further 5 minutes.

3 Lightly grease your baking tray or Swiss-roll tin. Place your dough in the tin and flatten it out, filling the tin evenly. Cover with a tea towel and leave it to rise again for 35–45 minutes until the dough puffs up a little.

Why? The dough needs a final rise so that it puffs up enough for you to make dimples in it.

Press the dough right into the edges – you may need to be firm as an elastic dough might spring back

4 Preheat the oven to 200°C (400°F/Gas 6). Scatter the remaining rosemary leaves and the pepper over the top of the dough. Poke the dough all over to make deep dimples, drizzle the remaining oil over, and scatter with the sea salt flakes. Bake for 15–20 minutes until browned.

Why? Dimples prevent the dough from rising up too much during baking.

To make dimples, poke the dough evenly all over with your fingertips

The perfect **Rosemary Focaccia**

The perfect focaccia will be lightly browned, evenly risen with a thickness of about 2cm (¾in), and will have a light and airy texture.

Did anything go wrong?

The focaccia hasn't risen very well. You may not have given the dough enough time to rise. The dough needs to be left to rise to allow the yeast to work properly.

The focaccia has risen unevenly. To avoid this, the dough needs to be evenly spread out in the baking tin.

The focaccia is very tough and heavy. You may not have kneaded the dough enough to allow the gluten to develop. Next time, knead your dough for as much as 10 minutes and ensure you really are stretching the dough.

The rosemary on top of the focaccia is burnt. The temperature of your oven may have been too high.

Crisp crust

Evenly spaced dimples

Light crumb

The olive oil will have soaked into the holes in the top of the focaccia and into the bread

Try more Yeast-risen Bread recipes ▶ ▶ ▶

White Loaf

1 loaf

Bakes in 40–45 minutes

Up to 4 weeks

Ingredients

500g (1lb 2oz) very strong white bread flour, plus extra for dusting

1 tsp fine salt

2 tsp dried yeast

1 tbsp sunflower oil, plus extra for greasing

MAKE THE DOUGH

Sift the flour and salt into a bowl. In a separate small bowl dissolve the yeast in 300ml (10fl oz) warm water and, once dissolved, add the oil to it.

Careful! Dissolve the yeast in lukewarm water – any hotter and it will kill the yeast.

Make a well in the centre of the flour, pour in the yeast mixture, and stir to form a rough dough. Bring the dough together, turn out onto a lightly floured surface and knead well for 10 minutes until smooth. Place the dough in a lightly oiled bowl, cover loosely with a clean cloth, and leave to rise in a warm place for up to 2 hours or until doubled in size. Turn the dough out onto the work surface and knock it back to its original size. Knead it until smooth.

SHAPE AND BAKE THE BREAD

Shape the dough into a long, curved, oblong shape known as a bloomer. Place on a baking tray, cover with cling film and a tea towel, and leave in a warm place for about an hour or until doubled in size. Preheat the oven to 220°C (425°F/Gas 7) and arrange the oven shelves so that there is one at the very bottom of the oven and one in the middle.

Slash the top of the risen loaf diagonally 2 or 3 times with a sharp knife – this allows the dough to continue to rise in the oven. Dust the top of the loaf with flour. Place the loaf on the middle shelf. Quickly place a roasting tin on the bottom shelf and pour some boiling water into it, and shut the oven door.

Why? Placing the tray of boiling water in the oven creates plenty of steam while baking, which helps the bread to rise and get a crisp crust.

Bake the bread for 10 minutes, then reduce the heat to 190°C (375°F/Gas 5) and bake for a further 30–35 minutes until the crust is browned and the loaf sounds hollow when tapped. Remove from the oven and leave to cool on a wire rack.

Walnut and Rosemary variation After the dough has been knocked back, gently knead in 175g (6oz) chopped walnuts and 3 tablespoons finely chopped rosemary. Halve the dough and shape each half into a 15cm (6in) round. Arrange on a baking tray, cover with a tea towel and leave to rise for 30 minutes. When the dough has doubled in size, brush with oil and then bake as in the recipe for 30–40 minutes.

Wholemeal Cottage Loaf

2 loaves

Bakes in 40–45 minutes

Up to 8 weeks

Ingredients

3 tbsp honey

3 tsp dried yeast

60g (2oz) unsalted butter, melted, plus extra for greasing

1 tbsp salt

625g (1lb 6oz) strong wholemeal bread flour, preferably stone-ground

125g (4½oz) strong white bread flour, plus extra for dusting

MAKE THE DOUGH

Mix 1 tablespoon honey and 4 tablespoons of lukewarm water in a bowl, then sprinkle the yeast over the top and leave to dissolve for 5 minutes, stirring once. In a large bowl mix the melted butter, yeast mixture, salt, remaining honey, and 400ml (14fl oz) lukewarm water. Stir in half the wholemeal flour with all the white flour and mix well. Add the remaining wholemeal flour 125g (4½oz) at a time, mixing well after each addition. The dough should be soft and slightly sticky.

Turn the dough out onto a lightly floured surface and knead for 10 minutes until it is very smooth and elastic. Place the dough in a lightly buttered bowl and toss the dough around to butter its surface slightly. Cover with a damp tea towel and leave in a warm place for 1–1½ hours or until doubled in size.

Why? Yeast works more efficiently in a warm environment, so speeding up the rising process.

SHAPE AND BAKE THE DOUGH

Turn the dough out onto the work surface and knock out the air. Cover and leave to rest for 5 minutes, then cut into 3 equal pieces; cut one of the pieces in half. Shape one of the larger pieces into a tight ball by smoothing it into a round, pulling any seams underneath the dough, and place seam-side-down on a lightly greased baking tray. Then shape one of the smaller pieces into a smaller ball, as before, and sit it seam-side-down on top of the first ball. Using your finger, press through the centre of the balls right down to the baking tray. Repeat this process with the remaining dough for the second loaf.

Cover the loaves with tea towels and leave in a warm place for 45 minutes or until doubled in size. Preheat the oven to 190°C (375°F/Gas 5). Bake the loaves for 40–45 minutes or until well browned. Leave to cool on a wire rack.

Remember When cooked through, the loaves should sound hollow when tapped on their base.

How to make **Pizza Dough**

Making deliciously light and well-risen pizza dough doesn't have to be a time-consuming task. Prepare the dough a day in advance and leave it in the fridge to rise overnight. The next day, all you have to do is roll it out – although the tricky part is achieving a good circle without knocking all the air out – before you top it and bake to perfection.

Tip The gluten in pizza dough gives it elasticity but sometimes makes it tricky to shape. If this happens, leave the dough to rest for 5 minutes, so the gluten relaxes, and try again.

Roll gently to avoid rolling out all the air pockets from the dough

Rolling out the pizza dough

On a lightly floured surface, gently stretch your dough into a rough circle. Using a rolling pin dusted lightly with flour, gently roll the dough from the centre of the circle in one direction only, giving it a 90° turn after each roll, until it forms a circle of your desired size.

Four Seasons Pizza

4 x 23cm (9in) pizzas

Bakes in 40 minutes

Unsuitable for freezing

Ingredients

3 tsp dried yeast

5 tbsp olive oil, plus extra for greasing

500g (1lb 2oz) strong white bread flour, plus extra for dusting

½ tsp salt

25g (scant 1oz) unsalted butter

2 shallots, finely chopped

1 bay leaf

3 garlic cloves, crushed

1kg (2¼lb) ripe plum tomatoes, deseeded and chopped

2 tbsp tomato purée

1 tbsp caster sugar

175g (6oz) mozzarella, thinly sliced

115g (4oz) mushrooms, thinly sliced

2 roasted red peppers, thinly sliced

8 anchovy fillets, halved lengthwise

115g (4oz) pepperoni, thinly sliced

2 tbsp capers

8 artichoke hearts, halved

12 pitted black olives

MAKE THE DOUGH

Dissolve the yeast in 360ml (12fl oz) lukewarm water in a bowl, then stir in 2 tablespoons of the oil. Sift the flour and salt in a separate bowl, add the yeast mixture, and combine to form a dough. Knead the dough well on a lightly floured surface for 10 minutes or until very smooth and elastic. Shape into a ball and place in a lightly oiled bowl covered with oiled cling film. Leave in a warm place for 1–1½ hours until doubled in size.

MAKE THE SAUCE

Melt the butter in a saucepan, add the shallots, 1 tablespoon oil, bay leaf, and garlic, and fry gently for 5–6 minutes, stirring occasionally so the shallots and garlic don't colour. Stir in the tomatoes, tomato purée, and sugar into the pan and cook for 5 minutes. Add 250ml (8fl oz) water, bring to the boil, reduce to a simmer, and cook for 30 minutes, stirring occasionally until reduced to a thick sauce. Press the sauce through a sieve, season, and chill.

Why? Sieving helps produce a smoother sauce, and it needs to be thick so that the pizza isn't wet and the tomato sauce doesn't dominate the flavours.

ASSEMBLE AND BAKE

Preheat the oven to 200°C (400°F/Gas 6). Transfer the dough to a floured surface and knead lightly. Divide into 4 balls and roll into approximately 23cm (9in) rounds. Place each round on a greased baking tray. Spread the sauce over the bases, leaving a 2cm (¾in) border around each. Divide the mozzarella evenly between the 4 bases. Place the mushrooms on a quarter of each pizza and brush with some olive oil. Place the pepper slices on another quarter and top with the anchovies. Top the remaining quarters equally with the pepperoni and capers and then the artichokes and olives. Bake 2 pizzas at a time in the oven for 20 minutes or until golden brown. Serve hot.

How to make **Sweetened Breads**

Sweetened breads such as fruit buns are made from yeast-risen bread dough enriched with butter, milk, and sugar. These additions give the breads a better flavour and softer texture. The rising of the dough, which may be a little softer because of these additions, is the secret to their success, giving them a beautifully light feel.

Making a well in the centre to add the yeast mixture makes mixing easier

Adding milk and yeast

For the dough to rise, you need to rehydrate or proof dried yeast by adding warm milk to it. Warm the milk gently until it is just warm enough for you to be able to put a finger in it – any hotter and it can kill the yeast. Then pour onto the yeast. Leave the mix to stand for 10 minutes until it becomes frothy. This is a good sign that your yeast is alive and active, before you add it to the other ingredients.

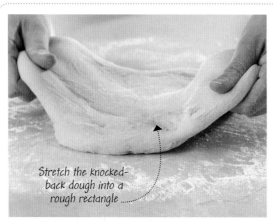

Stretch the knocked-back dough into a rough rectangle

Scatter the fruit on top, fold the dough over, and knead

Adding fruit

You add the fruit after the dough has risen once and been knocked back. At this stage, you shape the dough into a rough rectangle, scatter fruit on top, fold over, and gently knead in until the fruit is evenly mixed throughout. Then shape the dough, place it on a baking sheet, and leave to rise again for a final proof or rise before baking.

Spiced Fruit Buns

Makes 12

Bakes in 15 minutes

Up to 4 weeks

Ingredients

250ml (8fl oz) milk

2 tsp dried yeast

500g (1lb 2oz) strong white bread flour,
 plus extra for dusting

1 tsp mixed spice

½ tsp nutmeg

1 tsp salt

6 tbsp caster sugar

60g (2oz) unsalted butter, diced,
 plus extra for greasing

vegetable oil for greasing

150g (5½oz) mixed dried fruit

2 tbsp icing sugar

¼ tsp vanilla extract

MAKE THE DOUGH

Warm the milk gently until lukewarm, stir in the yeast, cover, and leave for 10 minutes until frothy.

Careful! Heat the the milk to a tepid or lukewarm temperature, any hotter and it will kill off the yeast.

Sift together the flour, spices, salt, and sugar, and rub the butter in (see p.26) until the mixture resembles fine breadcrumbs. Stir the yeast mixture into the flour mixture and bring together to form a soft dough. Turn the dough onto a lightly floured surface and knead well for 10 minutes. Shape into a ball, place in an oiled bowl, cover, and leave in a warm place to rise for 1 hour.

SHAPE THE DOUGH

Turn the risen dough onto a lightly floured surface, knock back, then shape into a rough rectangle. Scatter over the fruit, fold the dough over, and gently knead in the fruit until evenly mixed throughout.

Why? Knead the fruit into the dough only after the dough has had its initial rise, otherwise it will become too heavy to rise properly.

Divide the dough into 12 pieces, roll into balls, and place them spaced well apart on greased baking trays. Cover and leave in a warm place for 30 minutes or until doubled in size.

BAKE AND GLAZE

Preheat the oven to 200°C (400°F/Gas 6). Bake the buns for 15 minutes or until the buns sound hollow when tapped on their bases. Transfer to a wire rack to cool slightly. Before the buns cool completely, mix the icing sugar, vanilla, and 1 tablespoon of cold water together in a bowl, then brush over the still warm buns to glaze them.

Tip These buns will keep very well for up to 2 days if stored in an airtight container.

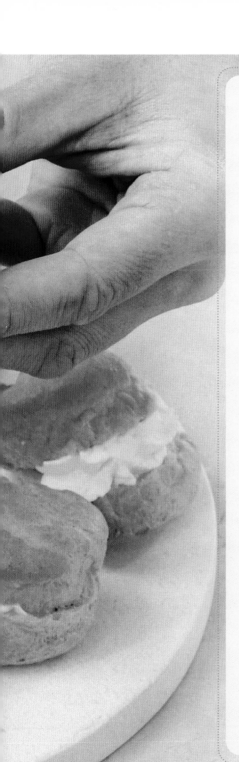

3

Take It Further

Take your baking to the next level with a final selection of recipes and techniques that will test and build on your new skills. Make sumptuous gâteau-style whisked cakes, learn how to roll and fold dough for light and buttery Danish pastries, and impress your friends and family with tangy artisan-style breads.

In this section, learn to bake:

How to make **Gâteau-style Cakes**

Gâteau-style cakes, which are usually layered with cream and fruit fillings, are the lightest cakes of all. Very little fat and no raising agent is added to these cakes, so it is vital to get a lot of air into the mix. This requires lengthy whisking, preferably over gentle heat, and careful folding in of the flour so air is not lost.

Whisk the mixture for at least 5 minutes or until the volume has trebled in size

Use a bowl that is larger than the width of the pan so the base doesn't touch the water, which would "cook" the mixture

Tip You can check if your mixture has enough air in it by doing the "trail" test: lift out the whisk beaters and if the drips from the beaters leave a distinct trail on the surface of the mix that doesn't disappear, then the mix is ready.

Whisking eggs and sugar

Over a pan of simmering water, whisk the eggs and sugar until very thick. Applying heat as you whisk helps to dissolve the sugar and slightly thicken the eggs, which encourages the eggs and sugar mixture to hold onto the air bubbles created.

Remember to scrape down the sides of the bowl

Do not overmix the cake mixture, otherwise the cake will be flat and heavy

Adding the dry ingredients

With a large metal spoon or spatula, use a figure-of-eight motion to fold in the flour. Firmly but gently, draw spoonfuls of the dry ingredients down into the wet mix and then turn the wet mix back over the dry. Repeat until no trace of the dry ingredients remains.

Use your hands to support the fragile cake layer as you cut it

Cut with a gentle sawing motion using a long-bladed serrated knife held horizontally

Cutting the cake into layers

Mark out the layers on the cake before cutting it. Don't rush and if it begins to slope, bring the knife back on course. The best way to move the layers, without them breaking, is to place both hands under each layer to support the cake slice and carefully lift into place.

Practise GÂTEAU-STYLE CAKES

Black Forest Gâteau

If any bake is sure to astonish and delight guests,
it's a creamy, layered gâteau. It might look tricky,
but just practise a few simple techniques and you
will achieve amazing results.

**Serves
8**

**Bakes in
40 minutes**

**4 weeks,
sponge
only**

Ingredients

85g (3oz) butter, melted, plus extra
for greasing

6 eggs

175g (6oz) golden caster sugar

125g (4½oz) plain flour

50g (1¾oz) cocoa powder

1 tsp vanilla extract

For the filling and decoration

2 x 425g cans pitted black cherries,
drained thoroughly and patted dry
on kitchen towel, 6 tbsp juice reserved,
and cherries from 1 can roughly chopped

4 tbsp Kirsch liqueur (or brandy,
if not available)

600ml (1 pint) double cream

150g (5½oz) dark chocolate, finely grated

Special Equipment

23cm (9in) round springform cake tin

piping bag and large star nozzle

butter

eggs

**golden caster
sugar**

plain flour

**cocoa
powder**

**vanilla
extract**

**black
cherries**

**Kirsch
liqueur**

**double
cream**

**dark
chocolate**

**piping bag with
star nozzle**

Total time *1 hour 30 minutes, plus cooling*

Prepare
10 minutes

Make
20 minutes

Bake
40 minutes

Decorate
20 minutes

1 Preheat the oven to 180°C (350°F/Gas 4). Cut a strip of parchment 4.5cm (1¾in) deeper than the tin's height for the sides of the tin. Fold 2.5cm (1in) along one long edge of the paper, cut snips in it at a 45° angle, and line the side of the tin with the snipped edge at the bottom; the parchment will extend above the rim. Place the tin on parchment, draw a circle around the outside, cut the circle and line the base with it. Set aside.

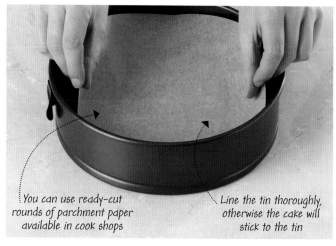

You can use ready-cut rounds of parchment paper available in cook shops

Line the tin thoroughly, otherwise the cake will stick to the tin

Whisk the mixture until it holds a trail that doesn't disappear when the beaters are lifted

2 Whisk the eggs and sugar in a bowl set over a pan of simmering water, until very thick and pale. Take off the heat and leave to cool slightly.

Careful! Keep the heat low and don't let the base of the bowl touch the water.

3 Sift the flour and cocoa together. Fold the dry ingredients into the whisked mixture very carefully so you don't knock any air out. Fold in the butter and vanilla extract.

Remember Fold very gently using a figure-of-eight motion to keep as much of the air you have just beaten into it. This will produce a light-textured sponge.

The batter is ready when no flecks of flour or cocoa are visible

4 Spoon the mixture into the cake tin, smooth over the surface, and bake in the centre of the oven for 40 minutes, or until well risen and just shrinking away from the sides. To test if the cake is done, insert a metal skewer into the centre of the cake. If it comes out clean, the cake is done; if not, simply cook for another few minutes and retest. Leave to cool slightly in the tin.

Level the surface with a spatula to prevent any peaking as it bakes

5 Transfer the cake to a wire rack and carefully remove the parchment paper. Leave to cool completely.

Why? Removing the baking parchment helps your cake to cool properly, and a wire rack allows air to circulate and steam to escape rather than condense as water, making the cake soggy.

6 Using a serrated knife, carefully cut the cake into 3 layers. Combine the reserved cherry juice and Kirsch liqueur, and drizzle a third of the liquid over each cake layer.

Careful! Make sure you drizzle the juice and liqueur mix evenly, otherwise parts of the cake could end up soggy, causing the sponge to collapse.

Divide the sponge evenly and keep the knife completely level

7 Whip the cream until it just holds its shape. Arrange one cake layer on a serving plate and spread with a third of the cream and half the chopped cherries. Repeat with the second layer, and top with the final cake layer.

Tip Divide the cream and cherries equally between the layers, but don't put on so much that the filling oozes out. A palette knife is the best tool to use here.

Carefully ease the layers on top, not pressing down as you could push out the filling

Coat only the sides with cream, making sure you don't get any on the top

Scatter grated chocolate onto a palette knife, then carefully press into the sides until all the cream is covered in chocolate

8 Spread the sides of the cake with some of the whipped cream. Using a palette knife, gently press the grated chocolate into the cream around the sides of the cake.

Careful! Spread the cream gently onto the cake sides, as you don't want any cake crumbs in the cream.

9 Place the piping bag in a jug or glass to support it, fold down the sides slightly, and spoon the remaining cream into the bag. Pipe rosettes around the edge of the cake by holding the piping bag over the cake, one hand at the top and one at the bottom, and gently squeeze the top of the bag until you've delivered a perfect cream swirl. Place cherries in the centre and sprinkle grated chocolate over the cream rosettes.

The cherries should be well drained, otherwise they will make the cake soggy

The perfect **Black Forest Gâteau**

The finished gâteau will be deliciously light and airy with mouthwatering layers of cream and cherries.

Finely grated chocolate tops the swirls of cream

Succulent layers of whipped cream laced with chopped cherries

Deliciously light and airy layers of sponge

Did anything go wrong?

The egg and sugar mixture looks like it has separated. Your bowl has touched the water in the pan underneath and caused the eggs to curdle.

The cake is very flat. You didn't whisk the egg and sugar mixture for long enough.

There are white specks in the cooked cake. You didn't mix in the flour properly.

The sides of the cake are wet. The cake has been left to cool for too long in the tin. Next time, let it cool in the tin for no more than 5 minutes, then transfer it to a wire rack.

The cake collapsed when I cut it into layers. The cake was warm when you cut it. Make sure it has cooled completely, as the cake is fragile when it is warm.

The cream has started to run off the sides of the cake. Your cake was not completely cool when you added the cream.

On cutting the cake the gâteau collapsed and the cream started to ooze out. You may have used too much force when cutting the cake. Next time, use a gentle sawing motion when cutting the cake into slices so you don't squash the layers together.

Try more Gâteau-style Cake recipes ▶ ▶ ▶

Génoise with Raspberries and Cream

**Serves
8–10**

**Bakes in
25–30
minutes**

**4 weeks
unfilled**

Ingredients

45g (1½oz) unsalted butter, melted, plus
extra for greasing

4 large eggs

125g (4½oz) caster sugar

125g (4½oz) plain flour

1 tsp vanilla extract

finely grated zest of 1 lemon

450ml (15fl oz) double cream

400g (14oz) raspberries, plus extra to decorate

1 tbsp icing sugar, plus extra for dusting

Special Equipment

20cm (8in) round springform cake tin

Preheat the oven to 180°C (350°F/Gas 4). Grease the
cake tin and line the base with baking parchment.

BEAT THE MIXTURE

Bring a saucepan of water to just below
the boil, then remove from the heat. Sit a large
heatproof bowl over the pan, ensuring the base
of the bowl doesn't touch the water. Add the
eggs and sugar to the bowl and, using an electric
whisk, beat for 5 minutes or until very thick
and the beaters leave a trail when lifted. The
mixture will increase up to 5 times its original
volume. Remove from the heat, whisk for a further
1 minute, and cool.

Sift the flour into the bowl and carefully fold
it in with the vanilla, lemon zest, and melted
butter, taking care you don't knock any air out
of the mixture.

BAKE THE CAKE

Spoon the mixture into the tin and bake for
25–30 minutes or until the top is springy and golden
brown. Test with a metal skewer and if it comes out
clean from the centre of the cake, it is done, and if
not, simply bake for another few minutes and test
again. Leave the cake to cool in its tin for 4–5
minutes as it is very fragile at this stage. Then turn
the cake out onto a wire rack, removing the baking
parchment, and leave it to cool completely.

Tip Run a knife around the edge of the tin before
removing the cake to ensure clean sides.

FILL AND SERVE

Whip the double cream in a large bowl until
it forms soft peaks. Lightly crush 325g (11oz) of the
raspberries with the icing sugar and fold into the
cream, leaving behind any raspberry juice so as
not to make the cream too wet.

Carefully cut the cooled cake into 3 equal
horizontal layers using a serrated knife. Place
the bottom layer on a serving plate and spread
with half of the cream mixture. Top with the
second layer and spread with the remaining
cream. Top the cake with the final layer, then
decorate with the remaining raspberries, and
a dusting of icing sugar before serving in slices.

Chocolate Amaretti Roulade

**Serves
6–8**

**Bakes in
20 minutes**

**8 weeks,
unfilled**

Ingredients

6 large eggs, separated

150g (5½oz) caster sugar

50g (1¾oz) cocoa powder, plus extra for dusting

icing sugar for dusting

300ml (10fl oz) double cream

2–3 tbsp Amaretto or brandy

20 Amaretti biscuits, crushed, plus 2 for the topping

50g (1¾oz) dark chocolate, grated

Special Equipment

20 x 28cm (8 x 11in) Swiss roll tin or deep baking tray

Preheat the oven to 180°C (350°F/Gas 4). Line
the base and sides of the tin or baking tray
with baking parchment.

BEAT THE MIXTURE

Bring a saucepan of water to just below the boil,
then remove from the heat. Sit a heatproof bowl over
the pan, ensuring the base of the bowl doesn't touch
the water. Add the egg yolks and sugar to the bowl
and, using an electric whisk, beat for 10 minutes or
until thick and creamy. Remove from the heat.

Whisk the egg whites in a separate clean bowl
with an electric whisk until soft peaks form. Sift
the cocoa powder into the yolk mixture, then
gently fold in with the whisked egg whites.

Careful! Whisk the egg whites in a clean, grease-
free bowl, otherwise they won't increase in volume.

BAKE THE SPONGE

Pour the mixture into the tin, smoothing it into
the corners. Bake in the preheated oven for 20
minutes or until just firm to the touch and a metal

skewer comes out clean. Leave to cool in its tin for at
least 5 minutes before turning out, face down onto a
sheet of baking parchment that has been dusted
well with icing sugar. Cool for at least 30 minutes.

Careful! The sponge must be completely cool
before filling, otherwise the cream will melt.

ASSEMBLE THE CAKE

Whip the double cream with an electric whisk
until it forms soft peaks. Trim the sides of the sponge
to neaten them, then drizzle over the Amaretto.
Spread the cream over the sponge and scatter with
the crushed Amaretti biscuits. Roll it up lengthways,
using the baking parchment to help keep it tightly
rolled. Arrange the cake on a serving plate with the
seam underneath. Crumble the remaining Amaretti
biscuits on top. Sprinkle with grated chocolate, dust
with icing sugar and cocoa, and serve in slices.

Tip To roll the roulade, hold the longest edge of the
parchment furthest from you and lift it up carefully.
Pull it towards you, and over the sponge as you roll
the sponge towards you. The parchment will help
to contain the sponge and shape it into a neat roll.

How to make **Choux Pastry**

Choux pastry is a very light and airy pastry made with egg that is used for baking profiteroles and éclairs. By beating enough air into the soft, doughy mixture you will guarantee crisp and light pastry that will rise beautifully as it bakes.

Beat the mixture with a wooden spoon until it forms a soft dough ball

Careful! Don't overboil the butter and water as this will cause the water to evaporate. You need the steam from the water to help the pastry rise.

Shooting in the flour

The traditional technique for beating flour into melted butter and water is called "shooting" the flour, meaning you add it all in one go. Sift the flour onto a piece of baking parchment, then tip it all into the pan – the flour cooks instantly and evenly. Then beat the mixture vigorously, but stop when it forms a ball of soft dough that comes away from the sides of the pan.

Add the eggs slowly to ensure a soft dough of pipeable consistency

Beat in the eggs using a vigorous action

Beating in the eggs

Using a wooden spoon, beat the eggs into the mixture a little at a time. Adding the eggs one at a time not only makes it easier to incorporate them into the mix, but with each beating you are also adding more air. The dough should now be soft enough to pipe.

Help! If your piped rounds peak up too much at their tips, simply press down lightly, using a dampened finger.

Make sure the rounds are all the same size to guarantee even baking

Piping the dough

Fit your piping bag with a plain nozzle and fill it with the choux dough. With one hand at the top of your piping bag and one at the bottom, squeeze the dough out from the top into even, walnut-sized rounds. Leave space in between each round for spreading and puffing up.

Practise CHOUX PASTRY

Profiteroles

Profiteroles are puffed buns made from smooth, pipeable
choux dough. Try this classic recipe for light, crispy
profiteroles, filled with cream and topped with
a delicious chocolate sauce.

Serves 4 | **Bakes in 22 minutes** | **12 weeks, unfilled**

Ingredients

60g (2oz) plain flour

50g (1¾oz) unsalted butter

2 eggs, beaten

For the filling and topping

400ml (14fl oz) double cream

200g (7oz) good-quality dark chocolate, broken into pieces

25g (scant 1oz) butter

2 tbsp golden syrup

Special equipment

2 piping bags, fitted with a 1cm (½in) plain nozzle and a 5mm (¼in) star nozzle

plain flour

unsalted butter

beaten eggs

double cream

dark chocolate

golden syrup

piping bags

plain nozzle and star nozzle

Total time *57 minutes, plus cooling*

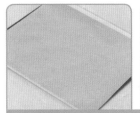   

Prepare
5 minutes

Make
20 minutes

Bake
22 minutes

Decorate
10 minutes

1 Preheat the oven to 220°C (425°F/Gas 7). Line 2 sheets with baking parchment. Sieve the flour into a bowl, then over a low heat melt the butter and 150ml (5fl oz) of water in a saucepan. Bring to the boil, remove from heat, and shoot in the flour all at once.

Remember To "shoot" the flour, transfer to a sheet of parchment after sifting into the bowl, then tip it into the saucepan all in one go.

Hold the sieve high to get as much air as possible into the flour

2 Beat the mixture together with a wooden spoon until it is smooth and forms a ball. Then leave it to cool for about 10 minutes.

Careful! Don't be impatient and add the eggs before the dough has had time to cool or you will start to cook them.

3 Gradually add the eggs, a little at a time, beating well after each addition until the eggs are fully incorporated.

Remember The more you beat the mixture, the more you develop the gluten and the more air you will get into it, helping the dough to puff up.

Add about a quarter of the eggs with each addition, beating well each time

4 Continue to beat the dough until you end up with a very smooth and shiny dough. Use a wooden spoon so you don't cut too much into the mixture, as this would break up the developing gluten and result in the buns not setting or rising well.

Remember The dough should be soft, not too sticky, and of a pipeable consistency.

5 Spoon the dough into a piping bag fitted with the plain nozzle. Pipe small rounds, set well apart, onto the sheets. Bake for 20 minutes until well risen.

Tip If you prefer your choux buns to have a more natural shape, use spoons to shape the dough.

Careful! Don't be tempted to open the oven too early or the buns may deflate.

Make sure you twist the top of the piping bag round to enclose the dough before piping

Flatten the tops of the dough balls by pressing down with a dampened finger

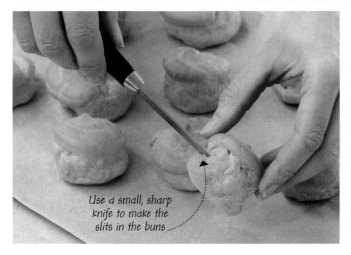

Use a small, sharp knife to make the slits in the buns

6 Remove from the oven, then make a 2.5cm (1in) slit in the side of each choux bun, allowing the steam to escape. Bake for another 2 minutes until golden brown and firm. Cool on a wire rack.

Why? You must slit the buns and let the steam escape, as steam will make them soggy. Work quickly so they don't cool too much.

7 Place 100ml (3½fl oz) of the cream in a saucepan, add the chocolate, butter, and syrup, and heat over a low heat until melted and smooth. Stir frequently to speed up the melting process.

Why? Heating the ingredients for the sauce over a gentle heat prevents the sauce from overheating and separating, also known as "splitting".

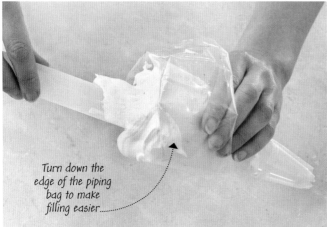

Turn down the edge of the piping bag to make filling easier

8 Whip the remainder of the cream until it forms soft peaks. The cream is ready if it holds its shape when the beaters are removed. Spoon the cream into the piping bag with the star nozzle, then twist the top of the bag round to enclose the cream.

Tip To support the bag and make it easier to fill, you could place it in a jug or tall glass (see p.52).

9 With one hand at the top of the bag and the other holding a choux bun, squeeze the cream through the nozzle and into the centre of the buns, making sure you don't overfill the buns. Arrange the filled buns into a neat mound on a serving plate, then spoon over the chocolate sauce and serve.

Tip Widen the existing slits in the buns with a sharp knife to make filling easier.

The perfect **Profiteroles**

Your finished choux buns should be light, crisp, and airy, and dry inside and out.

Chocolate sauce is smooth, rich, and glossy....

Softly whipped cream gives the perfect contrast to the crisp, light choux buns

Choux buns are light, airy, and golden ..

Did anything go wrong?

The choux pastry has cracks on the surface.
You may have beaten the dough for too long after adding the flour, causing the fat to separate, which leads to cracks on the surface of the baked buns. Next time, beat the mixture only until it comes away from the edges of the pan and forms a ball.

The choux buns are flat. You opened the oven door before the buns had properly risen.

The insides of the choux buns are soggy and still a bit doughy. Next time, remember to slit the buns with a knife and bake them until the insides are completely dry.

The cream filling is starting to melt.
You didn't leave the buns to cool completely before filling.

The chocolate sauce is granular. You may have melted the ingredients for the chocolate sauce over too high a heat, which can cause the ingredients to separate rather than amalgamate. Next time, melt them gently together.

The cream filling has started to run out of the profiteroles. The profiteroles may not have cooled enough before filling or the cream wasn't whipped enough. Next time, leave them to cool completely before filling and also whip the cream until it forms soft peaks and holds its shape.

Try more Choux Pastry recipes ▶ ▶ ▶

Chocolate Orange Profiteroles

**Serves
6**

**Bakes in
22 minutes**

**12 weeks,
unfilled**

Ingredients

60g (2oz) plain flour

50g (1¾oz) unsalted butter

2 eggs, beaten

500ml (16fl oz) double cream

finely grated zest of 1 large orange

3 tbsp Grand Marnier

150g (5½oz) good-quality dark chocolate,
broken into pieces

300ml (10fl oz) single cream

2 tbsp golden syrup

Special Equipment

2 piping bags fitted with a 1cm (½in) plain
nozzle and a 5mm (¼in) star nozzle

Preheat the oven to 220°C (425°F/Gas 7). Line
2 large baking sheets with baking parchment.

MAKE THE CHOUX PASTE

Sift the flour onto a sheet of baking parchment
or greaseproof paper.

Remember Lift the sieve high when sifting the
flour to get as much air into it as possible.

Melt the butter with 150ml (5fl oz) water in a
saucepan over a gentle heat. Bring to the boil,
remove from the heat, and immediately shoot the
flour into the pan. Beat with a wooden spoon until
smooth and the mixture forms a ball. Cool for 10
minutes. Slowly add the eggs to the pan, a little
at a time, beating well after each addition until
you have a stiff, smooth paste.

SHAPE AND BAKE THE PASTRY

Spoon the mixture into the piping bag fitted
with the 1cm (½in) plain nozzle. Pipe walnut-sized
rounds on the trays, leaving enough space in
between each bun. Bake in the oven for 20 minutes
or until well risen and golden brown. Remove from
the oven and slit the side of each bun carefully
with a knife to prevent it from getting soggy.
Return to the oven for 2 minutes to crisp up,
then cool completely on a wire rack.

FILL AND DECORATE

To make the filling, whip the double cream,
orange zest, and 2 tablespoons of Grand Marnier
together in a bowl using an electric whisk until just
thicker than soft peaks. Spoon the cream into the
other piping bag fitted with the 5mm (¼in) star
nozzle and fill each profiterole with the cream.
To make the chocolate sauce, melt the chocolate,
single cream, syrup, and the remaining Grand
Marnier together in a saucepan until smooth.
Arrange the filled profiteroles on a serving plate,
spoon the sauce over, and serve.

Tip The unfilled choux buns will keep well for
up to 2 days if stored in an airtight container.

Chocolate Éclairs

Makes 30 **Bakes in 25–30 minutes** **12 weeks, unfilled**

Ingredients

125g (4½oz) plain flour

75g (2½oz) unsalted butter

3 eggs, beaten

500ml (16fl oz) double cream

150g (5½oz) good-quality dark chocolate, broken into pieces

Special Equipment

2 piping bags fitted with a 1cm (½in) plain nozzle

Preheat the oven to 200°C (400°F/Gas 6). Line 2 large baking trays with baking parchment.

MAKE THE CHOUX PASTE

Sift the flour onto a sheet of baking parchment or greaseproof paper.

Remember Lift the sieve high when sifting the flour to get as much air into it as possible.

Melt the butter with 200ml (7fl oz) water in a saucepan over a gentle heat. Bring to the boil, remove from the heat, and immediately shoot the flour into the pan. Beat with a wooden spoon until smooth and the mixture forms a ball. Cool for 10 minutes. Slowly add the eggs to the pan, a little at a time, beating well after each addition until all are mixed to a stiff, smooth paste.

SHAPE AND BAKE THE PASTRY

Spoon the mixture into a piping bag fitted with the 1cm (½in) plain nozzle. Pipe 30 10cm (4in) lengths of the mixture onto the baking trays, cutting the end of the lengths from the bag with a wet knife.

Why? Using a wet knife to cut the pastry into lengths gives the éclairs a clean finish.

Bake the pastry for 20–25 minutes or until golden brown. Then remove from the oven and slit the side of each carefully with a knife to allow the steam to escape. Return to the oven for 5 minutes until the insides are dried out. Remove and leave to cool on a wire rack.

FILL AND DECORATE

Whip the cream in a bowl using an electric whisk until soft peaks form. Spoon the cream into the other piping bag, or reuse the first one, ensuring it is washed and dried first. Then pipe the cream into each éclair. Melt the chocolate in a heatproof bowl set over a pan of simmering water until fully melted and smooth. Spoon the chocolate over the tops of the éclairs, leave to set, and then serve.

Remember Do not let the bowl of chocolate come into direct contact with the water, otherwise the chocolate will overheat and become grainy.

Tip The unfilled éclairs will keep well for up to 2 days if stored in an airtight container.

How to make **Danish Pastry**

Danish pastries are made from sweetened, buttery layers of yeast-risen dough. Making the dough is the trickiest part, as you must knead, roll, and fold it a few times, incorporating butter as you go, to create light, flaky layers of pastry. Once you have made the dough, the fun part comes in shaping and filling the different types of pastry – and of course eating them!

Gradually draw in the dry ingredients into the yeast mix to make a rough dough

Careful! Make sure you heat the milk only until it's lukewarm, as too much heat can kill the yeast.

Make a well in the centre of the dry ingredients and pour in the yeast and milk mix

Adding the yeast mix

Dissolve and proof the yeast before adding it to the dough. Dissolving the yeast in warm milk ensures it's properly distributed throughout the dough. Proofing the yeast confirms it's alive, shown by a layer of foam forming on the surface of the yeast and milk mix.

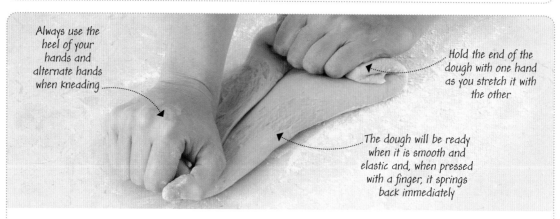

Always use the heel of your hands and alternate hands when kneading

Hold the end of the dough with one hand as you stretch it with the other

The dough will be ready when it is smooth and elastic and, when pressed with a finger, it springs back immediately

Kneading the dough

To develop the protein gluten present in the flour, which helps the dough to rise, knead the dough thoroughly for up to 15 minutes. Press the heel of your hands into the dough, then push it forwards away from you. Fold the dough back on itself after stretching, then give it a quarter-turn after two kneads, and repeat this process for 15 minutes.

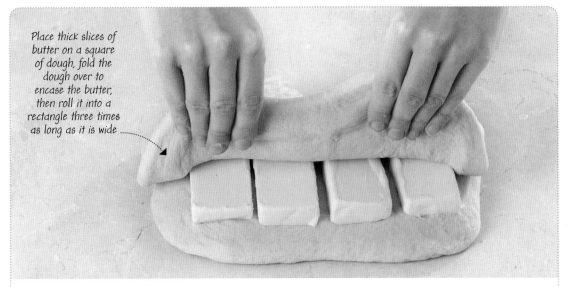

Place thick slices of butter on a square of dough, fold the dough over to encase the butter, then roll it into a rectangle three times as long as it is wide ....

Folding the butter in

The flaky texture of Danish pastry, which is sometimes called "laminated dough", is created by folding butter into the dough.

Distribute the butter evenly through the dough in layers, but ensure it does not melt, as this would make the dough very greasy.

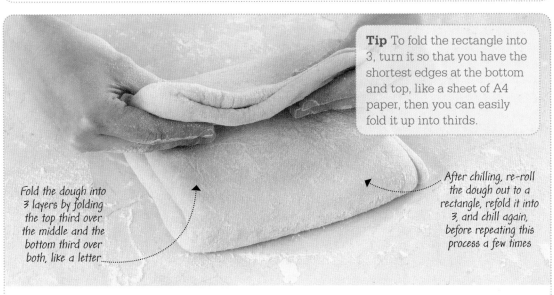

Tip To fold the rectangle into 3, turn it so that you have the shortest edges at the bottom and top, like a sheet of A4 paper, then you can easily fold it up into thirds.

Fold the dough into 3 layers by folding the top third over the middle and the bottom third over both, like a letter....

After chilling, re-roll the dough out to a rectangle, refold it into 3, and chill again, before repeating this process a few times

Folding and re-rolling

After folding the rectangle of dough into 3, it's important to chill the dough as this relaxes it, prevents it from shrinking, and

also stops the butter from seeping out. Always remember to roll the pastry in one direction, as this will distribute the butter evenly.

Danish Pastry

These Danish pastries are deliciously flaky and buttery,
and filled with a sweet jam or compote. Prepare the dough
the night before and keep it in the fridge ready to
roll and bake for a special occasion.

Makes 18   **Bakes in 15–20 minutes**   **Up to 4 weeks**

Ingredients

150ml (5fl oz) milk

2 tsp dried yeast

30g (1oz) caster sugar

2 eggs, beaten, plus 1 for glazing

475g (1lb 1oz) strong white bread flour, plus extra for dusting

½ tsp salt

vegetable oil for greasing

250g (9oz) chilled butter

200g (7oz) good-quality apricot, cherry, or strawberry jam or compote

milk

dried yeast

beaten eggs

caster sugar

strong white bread flour

salt

vegetable oil

chilled butter

apricot jam

Total time *2 hours 20–25 minutes, including chilling and rising time*

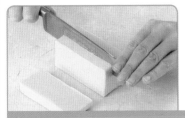

Prepare
5 minutes

Make *30 minutes + 1 hour chilling and 30 minutes rising*

Bake
15–20 minutes

1 Heat the milk very gently in a saucepan until lukewarm and no hotter, as too much heat can kill the yeast. Mix the warmed milk, yeast, and 1 tablespoon of the sugar together, cover, and leave for 20 minutes until frothy. Then beat the eggs into the yeast mixture. In a separate bowl, sift the flour, salt, and the remaining sugar and make a well in the centre. Pour in the yeast and egg mixture.

Your yeast mixture should look slightly bubbly and frothy after standing

Knead the dough by pushing it away from you, then folding it back on itself

2 Using a wooden spoon, mix all the ingredients together until they form a soft dough. Turn the dough out onto a floured surface and knead for 15 minutes. Grease a bowl with the oil, add the dough, cover with cling film, and refrigerate for 15 minutes.

Why? You need to chill the dough to help relax its gluten and so prevent the dough from becoming tough.

3 Roll the rested dough out by gently pushing the rolling pin across the dough's length. Give it a quarter-turn every few rolls and continue to roll until you have a square measuring about 25cm x 25cm (10in x 10in). Cut the butter into 4 even slices.

Careful! Ensure the butter slices are an even thickness as this is key to achieving even layers of pastry.

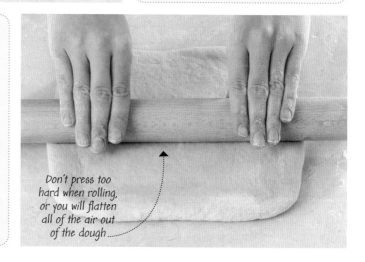

Don't press too hard when rolling, or you will flatten all of the air out of the dough

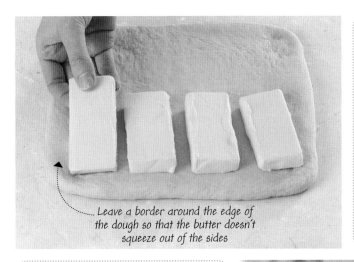

Leave a border around the edge of the dough so that the butter doesn't squeeze out of the sides

4 Lay the butter slices on one half of the dough, leaving a border of 1–2cm (½–¾in). Fold the other half of the dough over the top, pressing the edges with a rolling pin to seal.

Why? Sealing the edges of the dough contains the butter and prevents it from escaping when you start rolling out the dough.

5 Flour the dough and roll into a rectangle three times as long as it is wide and 1cm (½in) thick.

Why? You roll the pastry into a rectangle three times longer than it is wide so you can easily fold it into thirds.

Help! If your butter starts to break out of the dough, either at the sides or through the dough itself, simply chill for 15 minutes and try again.

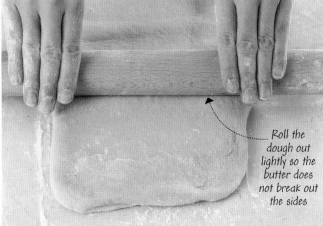

Roll the dough out lightly so the butter does not break out the sides

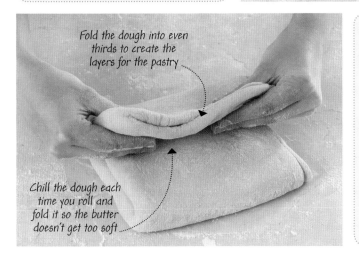

Fold the dough into even thirds to create the layers for the pastry

Chill the dough each time you roll and fold it so the butter doesn't get too soft

6 Fold the top third down into the middle, then the bottom third back over it, forming a neat rectangle. Wrap the folded dough in cling film and chill for 15 minutes. Roll it out again into a rectangle, as in step 5 and fold again before chilling for a further 15 minutes. Then repeat the steps – rolling, folding, and chilling – one more time. Always chill so the butter doesn't get too soft and the gluten relaxes.

7 Cut the dough in half, then roll each half out to a 30cm x 30cm (12in x 12in) square, 5mm (¼in) thick, by gently pushing the rolling pin across the dough and giving it a quarter-turn after every few rolls. Cut each square into 9 squares measuring 10cm x 10cm (4in x 4in) to give you a total of 18 squares. Make diagonal cuts from each corner to within 1cm (½in) of the centre.

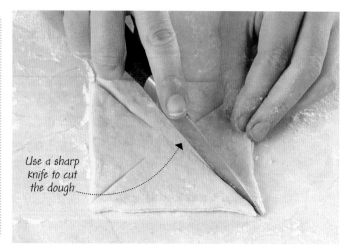

Use a sharp knife to cut the dough

8 Put 1 teaspoon of jam or compote in the centre of each square, and fold each corner into the centre. The jam or compote in the middle acts as glue to hold the pastry in the centre.

Careful! Don't overlap the corners of the pastry or the pastry might not cook through properly.

Make sure each corner doesn't overlap

9 Spoon more jam or compote into the centre of each pastry, and place on a baking tray lined with parchment. Cover with cling film and leave to rise for 30 minutes to set their shape. Preheat the oven to 200°C (400°F/Gas 6). Brush the pastries with egg wash. Bake for 15–20 minutes until golden brown.

Why? You brush the pastries with egg wash before baking to give them a beautiful glaze.

The perfect **Danish Pastry**

The perfect Danish pastry will be deliciously light and flaky with many layers and a beautifully soft texture.

Perfectly shaped pastries encase a golden pool of jam or compote

Light and flaky layers of buttery pastry

Did anything go wrong?

The Danish pastry is very flat. You may have rolled the dough out too thinly or left it to prove for too long, and the pastry collapsed.

The Danish pastry is far too greasy. Remember to chill the dough during the making, rolling, and folding stages, as insufficient chilling causes the butter to escape.

The Danish pastries have come apart on baking. You may not have left them to rest for the final time to set their shape before baking.

The Danish pastries are tough and hard. You may have overworked the dough and didn't leave it to rest for long enough.

The Danish pastries are very sticky and the jam has run over the edges. You may have put too much jam or compote in the centre causing it to run over the edges on baking. Next time, add just a teaspoonful to the centre once folded.

Try more Danish Pastry recipes ▶ ▶ ▶

Almond Crescents

| Makes 18 | Bakes in 15–20 minutes | Up to 4 weeks |

Ingredients

| 1 quantity Danish pastry dough (pp.171–73, steps 1–6) |
| 25g (scant 1oz) unsalted butter, softened |
| 75g (2½oz) caster sugar |
| 75g (2½oz) ground almonds |
| 1 egg, beaten for glazing |
| icing sugar, to serve |

Line 2 baking sheets with baking parchment.

SHAPE THE DOUGH

Roll half the dough out on a lightly floured surface to a 30cm (12in) square. Trim the edges to neaten, then cut into nine 10cm (4in) squares. Repeat with the remaining dough until you have 18 squares.

Remember Make sure your dough is thoroughly chilled when rolling out and cutting. This way it will hold its shape better.

MAKE THE FILLING AND ASSEMBLE

To make the almond paste, cream together the butter and sugar with an electric whisk, then beat in the ground almonds until smooth. Divide the paste into 18 small balls, and roll each one into a sausage shape a little shorter than the length of the dough squares. Place a roll of the almond paste at one edge of each square, leaving a gap of 2cm (¾in). Press it down and brush the clear edge with egg, then fold the pastry over the paste to incorporate it. Press the pastry down to seal.

Remember It is important to brush the edges of the dough with egg to ensure they are properly sealed. This will stop the filling from escaping through the edges of the pastry on baking.

Using a sharp knife, make 4 cuts in the folded edge of each pastry. Transfer to the baking sheets, cover, and leave to rise for 30 minutes in a warm place. Preheat the oven to 200°C (400°F/Gas 6).

BAKE AND SERVE

Form a crescent shape by bending the edges of the pastries. Brush with egg and bake in the top of the oven for 15–20 minutes, until crisp and golden in colour. Cool for 5 minutes on the baking sheet, then transfer to wire racks to cool completely. Dust with icing sugar and serve.

Careful! The baked crescents will be very fragile and should be left to cool down and firm up a little on their baking sheets before moving to wire racks.

Apricot Pastries

Makes 18

Bakes in 15–20 minutes

Unsuitable for freezing

Ingredients

1 quantity Danish pastry dough (pp.171–73, steps 1–6)

200g (7oz) apricot jam

2 x 400g cans apricot halves, drained

1 egg, beaten for glazing

Line 2 baking sheets with baking parchment.

SHAPE THE DOUGH

Roll half the dough out on a lightly floured surface to a 30cm (12in) square. Trim the edges to neaten, then cut into nine 10cm (4in) squares. Repeat with the remaining dough until you have 18 squares.

ASSEMBLE THE PASTRIES

Purée or sieve the apricot jam if it has lumps in it. Take 1 tablespoon of the apricot jam per square and, using the back of a spoon, spread it all over the square leaving a border of about 1cm (½in). Take 2 apricot halves and trim a little off their bottoms if too chunky.

Why? If the apricots are too chunky the pastry won't be able to wrap round and envelop them.

Place the apricot halves in 2 opposite corners of the square. Take the 2 corners without apricots and fold them into the middle to just partly cover the apricots. Repeat with the remaining dough and apricots until you have 18 pastries. Arrange on the baking sheets, cover, and leave to rise for 30 minutes in a warm place. Preheat the oven to 200°C (400°F/Gas 6).

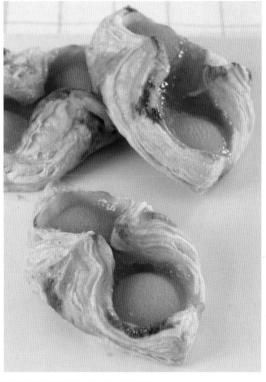

BAKE, GLAZE, AND SERVE

Brush the pastries with egg and bake in the top of the oven for 15–20 minutes until crisp and golden in colour. Melt the remaining apricot jam and brush over the pastries to glaze. Cool for 5 minutes on the baking sheet, then transfer to wire racks to cool completely.

Remember Make sure your apricot jam is smooth and lump-free before brushing over the baked pastries.

How to make **Artisan Breads**

Artisan breads are similar to yeast-risen breads, but use a different technique in preparing the yeast, known as "pre-fermentation". This gives the loaf a unique, slightly sour flavour and an interesting texture. A true artisan bread relies on cultivating the yeast naturally present in flour, so the following sourdough recipe is a bit of a "cheat's" version, as domestic yeast has been added. Different methods of pre-fermentation are known as a "starter" or a "sponge", each giving slightly different characteristics to the finished loaves.

The mixture will have increased in volume very slightly after fermenting

Stir the starter with a wooden spoon

As the yeast ferments, stir it once every day to ensure it doesn't end up in a solid mass

Tip To keep the starter active, healthy, and going indefinitely, stir it every 2–3 weeks to knock out the air, and also discard half of it, mixing in a fresh batch of 125g (4½oz) flour and 250ml (8fl oz) water. Do the same each time you use the starter to make a new loaf. Don't store it in high temperatures. Store it in a fridge, but bring back to room temperature before using.

Preparing the starter

Leave the yeast to stand or "ferment" in warm water and a little flour for 24 hours. Both the yeast and the bacteria naturally present during fermentation feed on the sugars in the flour, producing acidic by-products, giving the loaf its characteristic sour flavour. After 24 hours, by which time the mix will be a little frothy, stir the mix and leave to ferment for 2–4 days. The mix will produce more carbon dioxide, and it will look bubbly and develop a pleasant sour smell, vital for a good sourdough bread. The longer you leave it, the stronger the flavour of the bread will be.

Sponge will be well risen and slightly puffy in appearance when ready

More yeast is then added to the risen sponge with the strong white bread flour to form the baguette

Making a baguette sponge

A baguette's soft dough calls for a "sponge" method of pre-fermentation. Dissolve your yeast in warm water and a little flour, and leave it to rise for 12 hours. By leaving the sponge only for 12 hours, the gluten will not develop quite as much as in a sourdough starter, thus giving the baguette a slightly softer texture. The resulting sponge, which you mix with other ingredients, will also be slightly drier and firmer.

Starter should be bubbly and frothy

Mix until no flecks of flour are visible

Making an overnight starter

For an overnight starter, used in rye bread, mix the yeast with warm water, yogurt, and treacle, and leave it overnight, allowing the yeast to feed off the sugar in the treacle to produce carbon dioxide. It is now ready to be mixed with the other ingredients to make a dough.

Sourdough Loaf

You'll need to plan ahead for this deliciously tangy
sourdough loaf, as the recipe uses both a starter and
a sponge, requiring at least four days of pre-fermentation.
The unique flavour and texture of the loaf, however, will
be well worth the effort and if you keep your starter
going you can bake sourdough every day.

**Makes
2 loaves**

**Bakes in
40–45
minutes**

**Up to 8
weeks**

Ingredients

For the starter

1 tbsp dried yeast

250g (9oz) strong white bread flour

For the sponge

250g (9oz) strong white bread flour,
    plus 3 tbsp for sprinkling

For the bread

1½ tsp dried yeast

375g (13oz) strong white bread flour, plus
    extra for dusting

1 tbsp salt

vegetable oil for greasing

polenta or fine yellow cornmeal for dusting

a handful of ice cubes

Special Equipment

2 sheets of muslin

dried yeast

strong white bread flour

salt

ice cubes

polenta

vegetable oil

muslin

Total time *3 hours 5–40 minutes, including 2–2½ hours proofing time
and 4–6 days fermenting time*

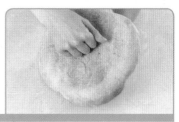

Prepare
4–6 days fermenting

Make *25 minutes*
+ 2–2½ hours rising

Bake
40–45 minutes

1 Make your starter 4–6 days before you want to bake your loaf by dissolving the yeast in a bowl with 500ml (16fl oz) lukewarm water. Stir in the flour, then cover, and leave to ferment in a warm place for 24 hours. Stir again, re-cover, and ferment for another 2–4 days, stirring every day.

Why? You need to stir your starter every day to prevent the mixture becoming a solid mass.

Starter should be frothy and have a sour odour after 24 hours

2 For the sponge, mix 250ml (8fl oz) of the fermented starter with an equal amount of lukewarm water in a bowl.

Why? Measure out only 250ml (8fl oz) of the starter, as it will have created more than this during fermentation.

Careful! Use only lukewarm water, or you will kill off the yeast.

Use only 250ml (8fl oz) of the starter

3 Stir in the flour, mix vigorously, and sprinkle with a further 3 tablespoons of flour. Cover the sponge with a damp tea towel and leave it to ferment overnight, once again, in a warm place.

Why? A damp tea towel creates the perfect moist environment for the yeast to continue developing.

Dough will be slightly sticky at this stage

4 To make the bread, dissolve the remaining yeast in 4 tablespoons of lukewarm water and mix it into the sponge. Stir in half the flour and salt, and mix well. Gradually add the remaining flour and mix to form a soft dough.

Why? Mixing the flour in 2 batches ensures the yeast and sponge are evenly distributed within the flour.

5 Knead the dough (see p.132) on a floured surface for 10 minutes until very smooth and elastic. Oil a bowl, place the dough in it, cover with a damp tea towel, and leave to rise for 1–1½ hours in a warm place until it doubles in size.

Remember Kneading helps to create gluten in the dough, allowing it to stretch as it rises. Without lengthy kneading your bread will be heavy and flat.

Dough is ready if it springs back when lightly pressed with a finger

Use your fists to knock the excess air from the dough by punching it

6 Turn the dough out again and knock back the dough to remove excess air. Cut into 2 equal parts, then shape each into a rough ball by pulling the ends into the centre underneath and pressing them together lightly to form a seam.

Why? Knocking back evens out the texture of the dough and redistributes the yeast.

183

7 Place each round of dough into a bowl, each lined with 2 pieces of muslin and lightly dusted with flour. Cover with a tea towel and leave to rise again for 1 hour in a warm place or until the dough fills the bowls.

Why? The muslin allows the dough to breathe and prevents it from sticking to the bowl. You can also leave the dough in an oiled bowl, covered with a tea towel.

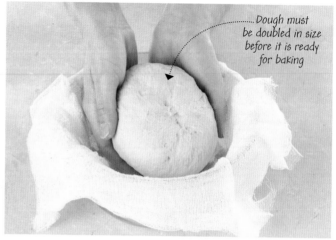

..........Dough must be doubled in size before it is ready for baking

Peel the muslin off carefully so as not to knock any air out ....

8 Preheat the oven to 200°C (400°F/Gas 6). Sprinkle 2 baking sheets with polenta, and place a loaf on each sheet, seam side down on top of the polenta. Peel off the muslin.

Why? Dusting your baking trays with polenta gives a nice, textured base to the loaf and prevents the bread from sticking.

9 Cut a cross on the top of each loaf so the dough relaxes and rises properly. Place a roasting tin in the bottom of the oven and put the ice cubes in it. Place the loaves in the oven, and bake for 20 minutes. Reduce to 190°C (375°F/ Gas 5), and bake for another 20–25 minutes until golden in colour.

Why? Ice cubes create plenty of steam in the oven, which helps the loaves develop a good crust.

The perfect **Sourdough Loaf**

The perfect sourdough loaf will be beautifully risen and golden in colour, with a chewy texture and a distinctive sour taste.

Crispy outer crust is golden brown in colour

Texture of the loaf is light, soft, and aerated

Loaf has a tangy, slightly sour flavour

Did anything go wrong?

The bread dough rose during proving but sank during baking. You may have forgotten to add the salt. During long fermentation, yeast can become very active, causing the dough to overprove, but salt will temper this behaviour. Salt also helps to create a stronger gluten network in the dough, improving the loaf's volume and preventing it from sinking.

The dough was too flat. You may have added too much liquid to the dough or you overproved the dough. Next time, leave the dough to rise until doubled in size and no more.

The bread is not crispy enough. You may not have built up enough steam in the oven. A humid environment makes the crust crisp. Next time, make sure you put ice cubes in a roasting tin or add more than you did last time.

The dough rose up too fast. You may have been working in a warm environment or used too much starter. Next time, you could leave the dough to rise slowly in a fridge overnight – that way it is easier to monitor.

The bread has a very soft crust. You may not have baked the bread for long enough. Make sure the oven is preheated at the correct temperature, and for an extra crispy crust, you can also spray the top of the bread with water before baking. To test if the loaf is baked to perfection, tap its base with your knuckles, and if it sounds hollow it is cooked through.

The flavour of the sourdough is too weak. You may not have left the mix to ferment for long enough. Next time, ferment for slightly longer.

Try more Artisan Bread recipes ▶ ▶ ▶

Artisan Rye Bread

**Makes
1 loaf**

**Bakes in
40–50
minutes**

**Up to
4 weeks**

Ingredients

For the starter

150g (5½oz) rye flour

150g (5½oz) live natural yogurt

1 tsp dried yeast

1 tbsp black treacle

1 tsp caraway seeds, lightly crushed

For the dough

150g (5½oz) rye flour

200g (7oz) strong white bread flour,
plus extra for dusting

2 tsp salt

1 egg, beaten, for glazing

1 tsp caraway seeds, to decorate

PREPARE THE STARTER

Begin preparing the starter a day ahead. Mix together all of the starter ingredients in a bowl with 250ml (8fl oz) tepid water. Cover and leave to stand overnight. The next day the mixture should be bubbling.

MAKE THE DOUGH

Mix the flours together with the salt, then stir into the starter. Combine to form a dough, adding a little extra water if needed. Turn the dough out onto a lightly floured surface and knead for 10 minutes or until smooth and elastic. Shape the dough into a ball, place in an oiled bowl, and cover loosely with cling film to stop the dough from drying up. Leave in a warm place for 1 hour or until doubled in size.

SHAPE THE DOUGH

Lightly knead the dough on a floured surface, then shape it into a rugby-ball shape. Transfer to a floured baking tray, re-cover it loosely, and leave to rise again in a warm place for 30 minutes. Preheat the oven to 220°C (425°F/Gas 7). Brush the dough with the egg and sprinkle over the remaining caraway seeds. With a sharp knife, make 3 slashes in the top of the loaf along its length: this will help the loaf to rise evenly in the oven.

BAKE AND SERVE

Bake for 20 minutes, then reduce the oven to 200°C (400°F/Gas 6). Bake for a further 20–30 minutes or until firm and dark golden in colour. The base of the bread should sound hollow when tapped. Transfer to a wire rack to cool.

Hazelnut and Raisin variation Don't use the caraway seeds. After the initial kneading, shape the dough into a rough rectangle, scatter 50g (1¾oz) each of toasted and roughly chopped hazelnuts and raisins on top of the dough. Fold the dough over and knead gently until the nuts and raisins are incorporated. Then shape and continue as in recipe.

Wholemeal Baguette

Makes 2 baguettes

Bakes in 20–25 minutes

Up to 4 weeks

Ingredients

½ tsp dried yeast, plus a large pinch for the sponge

1 tbsp rye flour

175g (6oz) strong wholemeal bread flour

vegetable oil for greasing

200g (7oz) strong white bread flour, plus extra for dusting

½ tsp salt

MAKE THE SPONGE

Prepare the sponge a day ahead. Dissolve a generous pinch of yeast in 75ml (2½fl oz) of tepid water. Add the rye flour and 75g (2½oz) of the wholemeal flour. Form a sticky, loose dough and place in a lightly oiled bowl. Cover with cling film and leave to stand for at least 12 hours or overnight.

MAKE THE DOUGH

Dissolve the remaining yeast in 150ml (5fl oz) tepid water. Put the risen sponge, the remaining wholemeal flour, the white flour, and salt into a large bowl. Pour in the dissolved yeast, and stir to form a dough. Knead the dough on a lightly floured surface until smooth and elastic. Put the dough in a lightly oiled bowl, cover with cling film, and leave for 1½–2 hours.

SHAPE THE DOUGH

Turn the dough out onto the floured surface and knock it back. Divide into 2 equal pieces. Knead and shape each into a rough rectangle, then fold both of the long sides into the centre and shape into a rounded oblong shape, pinching the edges together in the centre to seal. Then turn the dough over so the seam is underneath. Stretch and roll it into a thin, log shape, no more than 4cm (1½in) wide. Place on a floured baking tray. Cover with oiled cling film and a tea towel, and leave to prove until almost doubled in size. Preheat the oven to 230°C (450°F/Gas 8).

BAKE THE DOUGH

The dough is ready to bake when it is tight, well risen, and springs back on touch. Slash it diagonally all along the top using a knife. This will allow for the bread to rise in the oven. Dust the tops with flour, spray with water, and bake in the middle of the oven for 20–25 minutes. The bread will be ready when it is firm and the base sounds hollow when tapped. Remove from the oven and cool on wire racks.

White Baguette variation Make the sponge with strong white bread flour. Use 1 teaspoon dried yeast with 75g (2½oz) strong white bread flour for the dough.

Index